How to Behave So Your Children Will, Too!

A unique collection of practical strategies to
help parents discipline their children

Dr Sal Severe

Vermilion
LONDON

1 3 5 7 9 10 8 6 4 2

Copyright © Sal Severe, PhD 1997, 2000

First published in the United States in 1997
by Greentree Publishing, Tempe, Arizona

First published in the United Kingdom in 2000 by Vermilion

This edition published in the United Kingdom in 2004 by
Vermilion, an imprint of Ebury Press
Random House UK Ltd.
Random House
20 Vauxhall Bridge Road
London SW1V 2SA

Random House Australia (Pty) Limited
20 Alfred Street, Milsons Point, Sydney,
New South Wales 2061, Australia

Random House New Zealand Limited
18 Poland Road, Glenfield,
Auckland 10, New Zealand

Random House (Pty) Limited
Endulini, 5A Jubilee Road, Parktown 2193, South Africa

Random House UK Limited Reg. No. 954009
www.randomhouse.co.uk
Papers used by Vermilion are natural, recyclable products
made from wood grown in sustainable forests.

A CIP catalogue record is available for this book from the
British Library.

ISBN: 009188764X

Printed and bound in Great Britain by
Bookmarque Ltd, Croydon, Surrey

*To those who taught me the most
about good parenting:
my Parents, Mary and Tony, and
my children, Anthony, Leah, Alyssa and Dominic*

'Parents need to understand that their children's behaviour is often a reflection of their own behaviour. That's what makes this book unique. It does not focus on what children do wrong. It teaches parents what they can do differently.'

Preface

I have spent the last twenty-five years working with behaviour-disordered children. Some of these children exhibited emotional problems, learning disabilities and attention deficits. Most of these children were undisciplined, or rather, underdisciplined. They were all children who did not fit in because of the way they behaved. They did not fit in school or in the community. They did not fit in with other children.

Unfortunately, most of these children did not fit into their families, either. This was the problem I decided to resolve. I reasoned that working with parents had the greatest potential. Improve a child's family life, and all other aspects will improve as well. So I began sharing the experience I had learned within schools and treatment centres with parents. The results were amazing. Spending an hour a week with a child's parents was significantly more therapeutic than counselling the child for an hour.

I soon found myself working with groups of parents. Groups evolved into workshops. Since 1982 I have been conducting parenting workshops on discipline throughout the Southwest US. More than 12,000 parents have attended these workshops.

I believe that I have learned more from these parents than they have learned from me. Every time I heard a new idea or entertaining story, I would write it down. Every time I heard a solution to a common problem, I would write it down. This book is a collection of these stories, ideas and solutions.

~Sal Severe

Acknowledgements

Comments from colleagues are the strongest form of encouragement. I wish to express my sincerest appreciation to Jack Canfield for taking the time to read this book and for his guidance during the publishing process. Also, I would like to thank Dr Robert Brooks, Dr Neil Aaron, Marshall Langan, Mary Ann Perez and Cindy Wojtowicz for their kind remarks about this book.

Having ideas is one thing. Articulating them into print is another. I am most grateful to Dr Susan Krueger, Marge Scanlon and Bonnie Neal for their hours of proofreading and editing.

Thank you to the thousands of parents who have given me the positive feedback I needed to sit down and write this book. Above all, thank you to the parents and children who have shared their stories so that others may become better parents.

Contents

Preface | v
Acknowledgements | vii
About the Author | xi

Part I
Introduction | 1
Chapter 1 How Successful Parents Behave | 3
Chapter 2 Redefining Discipline | 13

Part II
How Children Learn Their Behaviour | 17
Chapter 3 How Children Model | 19
Chapter 4 You and Your Children Learn from Each Other | 23

Part III
How to Focus on the Positive Behaviour and Attitudes in Your Children | 31
Chapter 5 Spotlight Good Behaviour | 33
Chapter 6 Never Give Away the Ice Cream | 41
Chapter 7 Charts and Contracts | 49
Chapter 8 How to Use Rules and Consequences | 59

Chapter 9   How to Be Proactive | 63

Chapter 10   How to Motivate Your Children | 73

Chapter 11   Self-esteem: Motivation's Heartbeat | 81

Chapter 12   Being Consistent Can Make You Feel Dreadful | 87

Chapter 13   How to Be More Consistent | 97

Part IV

How To Manage Misbehaviour | 105

Chapter 14   How Children Learn to Misbehave | 107

Chapter 15   Why Children Push Your Buttons | 115

Chapter 16   Use Punishments That Teach | 123

Chapter 17   How to Punish Your Children Without
Punishing Yourself | 133

Chapter 18   Spanking | 147

Chapter 19   Correcting Misbehaviour with Time-Out | 147

Chapter 20   How to Manage a Child Who Refuses to Go
to Time-Out | 165

Chapter 21   How to Be Creative with Time-Out | 169

Chapter 22   How to Manage Arguments and
Power Struggles | 175

Chapter 23   Reducing Attention-Seeking | 187

Chapter 24   What to Do About Misbehaviour | 193

Part V

Dealing with Violence in Our Society and with Your Children | 197

Chapter 25   How to Raise a Nonviolent Child | 199

Chapter 26   How to Talk to Your Children About
School Violence | 207

Part VI

Simple Solutions to Prevailing Problems | 211

Chapter 27   Resolving Conflicts Among Siblings | 213

Chapter 28   Responsibility, Chores and
Pocket Money | 217

Chapter 29   Homework Hassles | 227

Chapter 30   Attention Deficits, Hyperactivity and Behaviour | 233

Chapter 31   Divorce | 237

Chapter 32   Peer Pressure | 249

Chapter 33   Hey, Teenagers! It is in Your
Best Interest To Behave | 259

Part VII
How to Enjoy Being a Parent | 263

Chapter 34   Promise to Appreciate | 265

Index | 271

About the Author

Dr Sal Severe is currently the Chairperson of the Psychological Services Department for the Cartwright School District in Phoenix, Arizona. He has been a school psychologist for 22 years. He has concentrated his practice on children and adolescents with emotional and behavioural disorders and their families. He has also worked as a teacher, counsellor, principal and director of special education. He has worked extensively with public and private schools including residential treatment centres. He has taught classes and has provided field supervision for school psychology internships for Arizona State University and Northern Arizona University. He has conducted training for the Arizona Department of Education.

Dr Severe is currently the President of the Arizona Association of School Psychologists and he is a member of the National Association of School Psychologists. Dr Severe has received the Golden Achievement Award from the National School Public Relations Association for his work in parent training. He has appeared on more than 300 television and radio programmes. Dr Severe and this book have been featured on the *Learning Channel's* programme, *Teacher TV*, MSNBC's *Daytime*, National Public Radio (NPR), the ABC Radio Network and Fox Network's *Fox on Family*. This book has been featured in Book of the Month Club and Children's Book of the Month Club. Dr Severe has provided parenting chats for America On-line and Parent Soup. Dr Severe is listed in *Who's Who*.

In the past seventeen years, he has conducted more than 500 workshops across the United States. He has become known for his work with schools, churches and parent organizations. He has provided training for The National Head Start Association, The National Association of School Psychologists, the Council for Exceptional Children, Tough Love, and the Haemophilia Association. Workshop themes include parenting skills, child behaviour, the effects of divorce on children, self-esteem, class-room management and instructional strategies. Dr Severe has provided training for the Intel Corporation, General Motors, SONY, Motorola, Honeywell, Texas Instruments, Pizza Hut, NAPA, Federal Express and Transamerica Occidental.

Dr Severe has four children who consume the remainder of his energy and time, but without reservation, provide him with his greatest blessing and achievement.

Part 1
Introduction

Chapter 1
How Successful Parents Behave

Whenever I am asked if my children have ever done something I was unprepared to handle, I tell this story. Anthony was almost three years old when my spouse became pregnant. We knew it was vital to prepare him for the arrival of a new baby. We wanted to avoid the dreaded effects of sibling rivalry. We read the *Berenstain Bears New Baby* book a dozen times. We did everything imaginable to make him feel that our new baby was also going to be his new baby. As Mum's tummy began to grow, Anthony kept a little doll tucked beneath the front of his T-shirt.

Leah's birth fascinated Anthony. He was so excited. Nearly everyone who brought a present for Leah brought one for him. It was like Christmas in May. He loved his new sister, even though he noticed that she did not have any teeth. Everything was going just as we had planned.

On Leah's sixth day home, it happened. Anthony hopped out of the bath. His rosy skin smelled like soap and baby powder. He asked if he could have an apple. I said sure. He reappeared a few moments later and placed one hand on the back of my chair while holding the apple in the other.

'Dad, I think I'm in trouble.'

'What for?' I asked.

'Well, when I was getting my apple, I accidentally "peed" in the fridge.'

'You're right,' I said. 'You are in trouble.'

What We Want

My children create many challenging situations. Occasionally I am amused. Often I feel frustrated and discouraged. Sometimes I feel embarrassed and guilty. Our children are a measure of our success and worthiness. We judge ourselves by their success and achievements. We compare ourselves to other parents, and compare our children to other children. Have you ever watched people buy apples? We rotate each apple looking for a blemish. We hold it up to the light, examining the reflection. We squeeze each one for firmness. We study each competitor looking for the perfect apple.

Parents want perfect apples. We want successful children, happy and well adjusted. We want them to feel good about themselves. We want children who are loving and respectful of others, well behaved, and self-motivated. We want them to be independent – not still living with us when they are thirty. All parents have the same goals and aspirations.

What We Have

Most parents confront the same behaviour problems. We become annoyed repeating everything three times. We spend too much time arguing. We become drained from the nagging and whining and manipulating and quarrelling, and exhausted from shouting and threatening. At times, it seems that all we do is punish. We feel guilty for getting angry, but it appears to be the only way to get results. We blame ourselves and feel ineffective for not knowing what to do. There are times when we dislike our children because their misbehaviour makes us feel so inadequate and miserable.

Raising well-behaved children is not easy. Many parents fail not because they are inadequate or because they lack love for their children or because they want something less than the best for their children, but because they are inconsistent. They procrastinate. They give warnings but do not follow through. They say things they do not mean. They lack patience. They punish in anger. Unsuccessful parents attend to the negative rather than the positive. They criticize too much. Parents who have discipline problems do not plan. They do not realize that they can be part of the problem.

Parents are part of the problem because of their *patterns of reaction*. Parents usually react in one of two ways. Sometimes parents react passively, they give in to misbehaviour because they do not feel like confronting the problem, at least not right then. You will learn why giving in makes misbehaviour worse. Sometimes parents react with anger. You can also learn how reacting with anger makes misbehaviour worse.

The way you react to your children's misbehaviour affects future misbehaviour. A certain amount of misbehaviour is normal; my guess is that young children misbehave about 5 per cent of the time. (Some days it feels like 50 per cent!) Knowing how to react to this 5 per cent is crucial. Reacting correctly and consistently can reduce misbehaviour from 5 per cent to less than 2 per cent, while reacting incorrectly can increase misbehaviour to 10 per cent or more.

Knowing how to react is essential, but knowing how to prevent discipline problems is more important. You can escape many predicaments by setting up a few guidelines in advance. Successful parents believe in prevention and planning; they are more proactive than reactive. You will learn several strategies to help you be more proactive.

What We Need

What factors contribute to successful parenting? Successful parents and their children are partners in discipline. Successful parents know that discipline is a teaching process, not just punishment. Successful parents understand that their behaviour and emotions affect their children's behaviour and emotions. Successful parents model responsibility; they focus their attention and energy on the positive aspects of their children's behaviour and emphasize co-operation, not control. Successful parents teach their children to think for themselves. They teach children self-control. Successful parents build self-esteem. They know that healthy self-esteem is the main ingredient children need to develop self-confidence and resiliency.

Successful parents learn from their children. They develop reaction patterns that reduce misbehaviour. Successful parents are consistent; they say what they mean and mean what they say. They follow through. Successful parents stay calm when their buttons are being pushed. They use punishments that teach, not get even. Successful parents connect special activities with good behaviour.

Successful parents anticipate problems. They have a game plan. They have proactive strategies for managing tantrums, disobedience, fighting, arguments and power struggles. Successful parents have plans that teach the value of completing chores, earning pocket money, and doing homework.

Successful parents do not let misbehaviour keep them from enjoying their children. Successful parents are strict but positive. They are serious about the importance of proper conduct, but they have a childlike sense of humour whenever it is needed. Successful parents know how to appreciate their children, even when they are misbehaving. Most importantly, successful parents are open to change.

How This Book Will Help

This book will make your life easier. This book teaches you how to get your children to listen the first time you ask them to do something. It teaches you how to be more consistent. It shows you how to get your children to behave without getting angry. It explains how to use incentives without bribing. It shows you how to use punishments that teach. It explains how to punish your children without feeling punished yourself. It teaches you how to correct your children without arguments and power struggles. It empowers you to handle teasing and tantrums. It will even tell you what to do when one of your children 'pees' in the fridge.

If you already have well-behaved children, thank your higher power. This book will help you too. It will make you more conscious of the successful strategies you are currently using. This book will show you how to maintain good behaviour, and it will prepare you for any future problems.

One of the best sources of help for parents is other parents. I realized this after watching parents who have attended my parenting workshops. It's thrilling to see parents pick each other's brains for techniques. They find ideas that will stop Jonathan's tantrums or get Heather to do her homework or get the twins to stop fighting. This book is a collection of ideas that I have learned from parents – parents who were fatigued and confused, parents drained by yelling, parents who felt imprisoned by their children, parents who walked through life on a treadmill, parents whose hearts were empty, parents who sometimes felt like giving up. Parents who discovered a better way.

All the examples in this book are true stories from actual parents with real problems. The ideas in this book are simple and practical. Everything is explained in down-to-earth language.

There are a number of theories about parent and child behaviour. Most authors accept one theory. They try to convince you that their ideas work for every parent and every child.

After trying this approach, I decided it was insufficient. Since every parent and child is unique, why not use a variety of methods? Use the best from every theory. This book provides hundreds of ideas. Not all of them will work all the time. You need to select the ideas that make sense to you.

How We Learn Parenting Behaviour

We learned most of our parenting behaviour from our parents. Have you ever said something to your children and then realized you heard these same words – 'Be careful or you'll break your neck,' 'Be quiet and eat' – when you were a child? We parent the way we were parented. We discipline as we were disciplined. Most ideas that we learned from our parents are helpful, but some are not. We pick and choose from these methods. Things we like, we use. Things we do not like, we don't use.

We also learn by watching other parents for good ideas and by talking with friends. We learn from their experiences, they learn from ours, and we share techniques that work.

We also learn by trial and error. Much of what we do with our children is based on our best guess at the time. Some things work; some fail. This happens to us all. Every firstborn child is a test; we begin using trial and error the moment we get home from the hospital. I remember feeling confused and helpless. The baby is crying – what does it mean? Hungry? Lonely? Wet? Too warm? Too cold? Trial and error also applies to discipline: if sending your child to bed early works once, you will probably do it again.

The beliefs that you already have about parenting and discipline are fine. Learning from your parents and friends and learning by trial and error is normal. Add judgment and common sense, and you have a solid foundation. This book will build on that foundation.

Love Does Not Always Light the Way

Too many parents have the false belief that if they love their children as much as possible, their misbehaviour will someday improve. Love, warmth and affection are essential. They are fundamentals. But you also need knowledge.

Imagine you needed an operation. As you were about to be put under, your physician whispered in your ear, 'I want you to know that I am not a surgeon. I'm not a doctor at all. Please don't worry. My parents are both doctors. I have a lot of friends who are doctors. I've asked a lot of questions about surgery. Just relax! I have a lot of common sense, and I love my patients very much.' Would you let this person use a scalpel on you?

Parents need training just as professionals need training. Children need trained parents as much as they need loving parents. Training pulls together all the good ideas you already have, provides structure and direction, and gives you confidence. You learn that what you are doing is right. More confidence means more self-control, less anger, less guilt, and less frustration. More confidence means more respect from your children. Without confidence, many parents are afraid to correct or punish their children. Some worry that their children will not like them, or are afraid they might harm their children emotionally, so they let their children misbehave.

It Wasn't Like That When I Was Growing Up

Why doesn't discipline work the way it did twenty or thirty years ago? Why don't the old-fashioned methods work? Why is being a parent so demanding and confusing? Parenting is more difficult because childhood is more difficult. Children are under pressure – pressure to make adult decisions with the experience and emotions of a child; pressure from peers; pressure from school; pressure from the media; pressure that seeps down from pressures on the parents. Pressure on our children translates into problems for us.

Several changes in our culture have had a tremendous impact on discipline and our roles as parents. Our economy has created financial tension in families. Parents come home stressed. Their fuse is short. The rising divorce rate affects all of our children; today, there are schools where four out of five children have experienced divorce. Single parenting is stressful.

Twenty years ago, everyone in the same town or neighbourhood had the same values and beliefs. No matter where you went to play, the rules were the same. Everyone's parents had the same expectations. This is no longer true. Every family has its own standards. Our children experience many versions of right and wrong. This is confusing to children.

How do these changes in our society affect the way you discipline your children? Why won't the old ways work today? The old ways were simple solutions for a society with simple problems, but today's problems are more complicated. They require refined solutions. Our children live in the future, not the past. We have to cope with the adversity of our times. If you want to be a successful parent, you have to know how to discipline today's children. Parents need training – not because parents are incapable, but because parenting is no longer simple.

Three Successful Promises

There are three promises that every parent needs to make to become more successful. Promise to have courage to be open and accept new ideas. If what you are doing is working, stick with it. If not, then have the courage to try something new.

Promise to have patience – plenty of patience. If your child is twelve years old, he has had twelve years to develop his behaviour patterns. Give your child time to change. This is where most parents fail. We have gone from one-hour dry cleaning to one-hour photos to one-hour glasses to thirty-minute tune-ups.

Microwave dinners, car phones, and fast lanes on motorways have conditioned us to expect instant gratification. Technology has taught us impatience. We believe that because we are trying a new idea, changes should take place overnight. A few days is not long enough to test a new idea. Some methods take weeks to show improvement. Be patient.

Promise to practise. Every parent must practise, even me. My children do not care one bit that I am a school psychologist who teaches parenting classes. When I'm home, I'm Dad. I get tested just like you. I have to practise, too. If you are willing to read about new ideas but not to practise them, give this book to someone else and buy a magic wand.

Children learn good behaviour as well as misbehaviour. Behaviour does not occur by magic. It is not inherited. A well-behaved child is not the result of luck. Be encouraged – if children learn behaviour, then children can learn to change behaviour. Parenting behaviour is also learned. Good parenting skills do not appear suddenly and instinctively. You can learn to be a more successful parent.

This is a book about parent behaviour. It teaches you to examine your own behaviour and determine when you are part of the problem, prepares you to support yourself when your children tell you they hate you, and shows you how to stay calm when your buttons are being pushed. This book enables you to build healthy self-esteem in your children, teaching them to think for themselves and withstand peer pressure. It teaches you how to enjoy being a parent.

If you are in pursuit of well-behaved, well-adjusted children, you need to understand how your behaviour is connected to your child's behaviour. I hope to teach you how to behave so your children will, too!

Changing Your Behaviour: Where to Begin

As you read the ideas in this book, you may think, 'Sounds great. That will really work for me.' But reading about a new technique is not the same as practising a new technique. Practising a new idea means changing your behaviour. Any change in behaviour means changing habits, and habits are not easy to change. Old habits are more comfortable than new ones.

As you continue with this book, you will be learning about successful parent behaviours, reading about strategies and techniques that you need to use more, and behaviours that are counterproductive. You will need to cut down on these behaviours. You will also find that many of your present ideas are appropriate and need no change. As you read, make a list of behaviours that you need to practise more, behaviours you need to practise less, and behaviours that are appropriate and should be continued.

Since it takes about a month to develop new habits, review your list two or three times a week for the next four weeks. This review will help you solidify your new habits more quickly.

Behaviour I need to practise *more.*

_____

_____

_____

_____

Behaviour I need to practise *less.*

_____

_____

_____

_____

Behaviour that is appropriate, which I need to *continue.*

_____

_____

_____

_____

Chapter 2
Redefining Discipline

'How do you discipline your children?'
'I scream a lot.'
'Does that work?'
'Not usually. They might settle down for a few
    minutes.'
'Then what?'
'They start fighting again.'
'What do you do then?'
'I get mad and give each of them a spanking.'
'Does that stop them?'
'For a little while.'

When I ask parents how they discipline their children, most parents tell me how they punish their children. They yell, scold, spank, take privileges away, and restrict their children to their bedrooms. Discipline and punishment are not the same. When used correctly, punishment is a small part of the total discipline process.

Discipline includes all those things that we do as parents to teach our children how to make better decisions. Discipline is teaching children how to make better choices about their behaviour. Discipline is teaching children to be responsible. Discipline is teaching children to think for themselves. Discipline is teaching children that they have the power to choose how they behave. These definitions are completely different from the belief that discipline is punishment. *Discipline means teaching decision making.*

Emphasize Co-operation, Not Control

Many parents are confused about the purpose of discipline. They believe the purpose of discipline is to control a child's behaviour – make him behave no matter what. This goal is unreasonable and unattainable. The purpose of discipline is not control, but co-operation. Co-operation means that your children choose to behave because it makes sense to behave. It feels good to behave. This is the goal of good discipline. Unfortunately, many parents spend hours each day chasing their children around the house trying to make them behave.

Discipline should not be a negative force that brings bad feelings to everyone involved. The thought of disciplining your children should not upset your stomach. I knew a father who became so angry with his children he began taking tranquilizers.

Imagine that your daughter makes a mess in the kitchen. The former view of discipline would cause you to think, 'How should she be punished so she will not do it again?' You may get angry, yell or reprimand. You may spank her or send her to her room. The chances are that both of you end up feeling annoyed.

Discipline should instead provide your children with learning experiences. Think, 'What can I do so that she learns from this; so that she chooses not to do this again?' You want your daughter to clean up after herself. Say, 'Elena, I'm glad to see that you are old enough to make your own lunch. But I am disappointed that you left a mess. I know you can do better. Please go and clean it up. Let me know if you need help.'

There is an important difference between these two strategies. In the first case, you are trying to control your child's behaviour. The new approach encourages your child to control her own behaviour. This strategy makes more sense. Seeking control is seldom a better tactic than seeking co-operation. Once you believe that discipline is teaching decision making, you and your children will have an improved, co-operative attitude about discipline.

Are there ever circumstances when you should control your children? There are occasions, particularly with younger children, when you need to control. Your two-year-old daughter wants to play with an electric wall socket. You would control her by removing her from the situation. You decide for her. If you have a son who refuses to go somewhere with you, it is acceptable to take his hand and go. If your teenager drives carelessly, you would take away the car keys until he demonstrates safer habits.

The need for co-operation becomes more apparent as children grow older. You have less control over their behaviour, so you must rely on co-operation and trust. I once worked with a father who insisted that his fourteen-year-old son stay in the house after dinner. The opposition and resistance between father and son grew to the point of hatred. Dad installed an expensive burglar alarm to keep his son from going out of the bedroom window as a last, desperate attempt at control. All it did was challenge the boy; it took him four days to figure out how to deactivate the alarm.

Attempts to control teenagers are futile. You must depend on your teenagers to co-operate with your ideas of right and wrong. You must count on them to make their own decisions. Teenagers need to think for themselves, so when they face a strenuous choice, they will ask, 'Is this good for me?' Think of it this way. If your teenage daughter chooses to have sex, will she ask your permission? If your adolescent son decides to try pot, will he ask you first? Not likely.

How to Give Children Choices

Some parents make too many decisions for their children. They want to protect their children from making a wrong choice and to safeguard them against painful outcomes. This is understandable, but it denies your child opportunities to learn. Making choices for your children may give them the message that they are incapable of making their own decisions. Use judgement and caution without being overprotective. Think about your child's choices, rules and activities in three ways. Some things are required: passing exams, helping around the house. Some things you will negotiate: what time to come home, TV programmes, make up, snacks. Give them full authority in some choices: sports, music, school activities. As children mature and show more responsibility, gradually allow them more authority over their lives. If you expect more responsibility from your older children, give them more privileges; higher expectations need a higher incentive. Allow older children a later bedtime, more pocket money, more activities. This encourages them to continue to behave responsibly and make good decisions. It gives them confidence. They see you are a fair person so they will trust you. There is more specific information about this in chapter 28.

Discipline is teaching children to make decisions. The purpose of discipline is teaching children to be co-operative. Begin emphasizing co-operation and responsible decision making at an early age. Have faith in your child's willingness to co-operate.

Children are either in control or under control. Discipline means teaching children to control themselves. If you want your children to be responsible decision makers, you must teach them self-control. If you force control, they do not learn to master being *in* control; they do not develop self-control skills and habits, and as a result, they are out of control.

Part II
How Children Learn Their Behaviour

Chapter 3
How Children Model

Children learn by copying. A child's potential to observe and imitate is a remarkable quality. Scientists refer to this as modelling. Children learn to speak by modelling – by listening, observing and imitating. Children also learn attitudes, values, personal preferences, and even some habits by modelling.

Since children copy the behaviour of the people around them, you have a powerful influence on your children's learning. Think carefully about your behaviour. What you say and do in front of your children influences their thinking and behaviour. You are their model.

Anthony was five. He and I went Christmas shopping. The car park was jammed; we drove around for several minutes looking for a place to park. I am not blessed with patience in these situations. Finally I spotted a car pulling out. I drove up and put on my signal, indicating my intent. As the car backed out, another car sneaked in ahead of me. I got so angry. I rolled my window down and yelled something obscene at the driver. We exchanged a few angry looks, and then I continued my search for another parking place.

About twenty minutes later, Anthony and I were walking around the shops. I had cooled off. We were discussing what presents to buy. Without warning, he looked up and asked, 'By the way, Dad, what is an a——h——anyway?'

I felt as if I had been hit with a brick. What a shocking insight! He clearly heard me use bad language, and he remembered exactly what I said. I was so embarrassed. I explained that it was not a nice word and I was wrong for saying it. I admitted that I was angry and frustrated because I could not find a parking place. I added that I hoped he would not use the word as I did. It was a moment of truth for me.

You can be a good example to your children 95 per cent of the time. Isn't it fascinating how children always seem to catch you when you make mistakes? When children catch them misbehaving, many parents get defensive: 'Never mind what that word means. Don't ever let me hear you say it.' This response is wrong. It closes communication. It tells your child that you can say bad words but he cannot. The first thing your child will do when he gets to school the next day is start asking all his classmates what the word means.

How to Be a Good Model

Do not get defensive when your child catches you misbehaving. Take advantage of this situation. Turn your discomfort into a valuable learning opportunity. When I was caught using a bad word, I explained that I was wrong. I made a mistake. I was angry. I took responsibility for my anger. I did not blame the person who took the parking place. I admitted my error. I apologized. What am I modelling now? Parents make mistakes. When I do, I admit it. I take responsibility. I apologize. These are invaluable qualities to model for your children.

Children learn from everything you do. If you lie about your twelve-year-old's age to avoid the extra price of an adult ticket, you teach your child that lying is okay. If you tell the person on the phone that your husband is not home when he is, you teach your children that lying is okay. If you eat junk food, you teach your children to eat junk food. If you watch TV all day, you teach your children to watch TV all day. If you argue, yell, or call people names, you teach your children these things. If you get angry at your children, you can expect them to get angry at others. If you yell something obscene at someone who takes your parking place, you teach your children to use obscene language.

When you speak in a calm voice instead of an angry one, you teach your children how to stay calm when provoked. When you apologize for using bad language, you teach your children to take responsibility for mistakes. When you take responsibility for your anger, you teach your children to take responsibility for their anger. When you use polite language, you teach your children to be polite. When you share, you teach your children to share. When you are kind to others, you teach your children kindness. When you do your best, you teach your children to do their best. When you read a book, you teach your children proper attitudes about reading. When you eat healthy foods and take exercise, you teach your children to eat healthy foods and take exercise. When you behave in a responsible manner, you teach your children to behave in a responsible manner.

A horrible example of the effects of modelling is the epidemic of child abuse. Often, abusive parents were abused as children. When a violent and angry parent beats a child, the child learns that this is the way parents treat their children. When that child grows up, he will often treat his children the same way.

If your child's behaviour concerns you, look closely at your own behaviour. Children learn what they live. When they live with responsible parents, they become responsible children. They will grow up to be responsible parents to your grandchildren. You have an obligation to be the best model that you can be. Always. Your children do as you do.

Children Learn from Their Surroundings

A second way that children learn is by experiencing things in their surroundings. Your child's surroundings contain you and other family members, playmates, people in the neighbourhood, classmates, teachers, the lunchroom, the playground, TV, films, books, magazines, music, and so on. These are the ingredients of your child's environment – the world that surrounds him. Learning by experience is different from copying. If a child touches hot food, he learns that hot food hurts fingers. The child learns about hot food through experience, not by modelling.

Children behave to fit into their environment. If the environment rewards playing with dolls, children play with dolls. If the environment rewards playing football, children play football. If the environment rewards belonging to a gang, children join gangs.

The environment shapes your child's learning and behaviour. Parents who value education have children who do well in school. Families that encourage teamwork have co-operative, hardworking children. Neighbourhoods that foster harmony have children who play together nicely.

Your children copy what you say and do. They learn many of their behaviours from you; be a good example, and provide experiences that teach your values and encourage self-discipline and responsibility.

Chapter 4

You and Your Children Learn from Each Other

Every time four-year-old Michael goes to the supermarket with his mother, Connie, he asks for a chocolate bar. Connie says no. A few minutes later, Michael begins pleading for a chocolate bar. Connie still says no. By the third aisle, Michael is starting a tantrum. His begging escalates into demanding. Connie still says no. His face gets red. He kicks his feet and shakes the shopping trolley. Connie threatens to spank him if he does not stop. He doesn't. As they reach aisle 5, Michael's tantrum explodes. Connie looks for a place to hide, but she is in frozen foods. Tears! Screams! Kicking and shaking. Everyone is staring. Connie can take no more. She gives in. She buys the bar of chocolate.

Connie has taught Michael three things. She has taught him that the word *no* is meaningless. Connie's responses were: no, no, no, no, yes. That means that when Connie says no she does not mean no. She means, ask again and again, and get more

23

demanding each time. When your behaviour becomes so obnoxious that I cannot stand it any more, I will change my no to yes. It's like magic! No becomes yes! Connie has taught Michael to be persistent in a negative way.

Connie has taught Michael how to have tantrums. She has not done this on purpose, but she has done it. She has taught Michael that screaming and demanding pays off. If you scream and yell loud enough and long enough, you can get a chocolate bar. A chocolate bar is your reward. Have a tantrum – get a chocolate bar. Have a tantrum – get your way.

Connie has taught Michael that she does not mean what she says. She makes threats but does not follow through. She told him to be quiet or she would spank him. What did she do instead? She bought him a chocolate bar. Here is what Michael might be thinking. 'Well, I got my Snickers bar in aisle 7 this week. Last week it was aisle 8. I'm doing better. I love it when Mum gives me the "quiet or I'll spank you" routine. That had me worried the first time I heard it. That was two years ago, and she hasn't followed through yet. Maybe next week I'll try for aisle 5.'

Michael has taught Connie a few things, too. He has taught her how to gain peace and quiet and stop the embarrassment: Buy the chocolate bar. All Connie's other attempts at quietening Michael were futile: she could only achieve peace with chocolate. This has happened before. A pattern has been established. It will happen again. Giving in to Michael's demands is the only way to have peace and quiet.

There are parents who live every day of their lives in this way. They believe that giving in to demands is the only way to stop the tantrum. *This is a big mistake.* Reward a child's tantrum once, and you will be teaching your child to have more tantrums in the future. Give in to your child's shouted demands once, and you will be listening to shouted demands again and again.

What can you do if you are already trapped in this dilemma? Here is a plan that quietened the supermarket battleground. Connie stopped taking Michael on long shopping trips. She began by taking him on short trips to the local shops. Before they left the house, Connie would explain how she wanted Michael to behave. Connie would explain where they were going and what they were going to buy. She would show Michael the shopping list with three or four items on the list. At the bottom of the list, Connie would write a treat, such as biscuits. She would often ask Michael what he wanted to put on the list. She would let Michael hold the list while they shopped. This gave Michael ownership in shopping. It gave him something to do. It gave him something to control. As they obtained each item, he would cross the item off the list. If Michael did a good job, he could choose the biscuits.

> 'Michael, you and I are going shopping. I want you to listen to me while we are at the shop. I do not want any fuss. You can help me by holding the shopping list. You can cross out the items as we put them in the basket. If you help and do as I ask, you can choose the biscuits. I know you can do it.'

I explained to Connie that while they were shopping she would need to be generous with encouragement: 'You are doing a good job of checking the list. Thank you.' 'You are waiting nicely. Thank you, Michael,' 'I appreciate your help.' After two weeks of practice and a few minor setbacks, the plan proved to be working.

As Connie and Michael became more familiar with the rules of shopping, they took their plan back to the supermarket. Connie began with quick trips and short lists. This strategy eased the transition from the local shop to the supermarket. Gradually, she was able to extend her shopping time. Michael had learned how to behave. So had Connie.

Here is an example of a child who does not listen. Brad is an active and curious twelve-year-old. Most of the time, Brad's behaviour is fine. About once or twice a day, Brad becomes a little too excited, active, and loud. His father, Richard, always begins by calmly and politely asking Brad to settle down and play more quietly. Brad always responds to this initial request in the same way. He ignores Dad completely. The next round occurs a while later. Richard raises his voice: 'Be quiet, or you will go to your room!' Brad responds, 'Okay, Dad.' Brad makes no real effort to be quiet. Finally, Richard becomes angry and starts yelling. 'If you are not quiet right now, I am getting out the paddle.' This time, Brad becomes quiet and remains so for several hours.

Let's examine what Richard and Brad have learned from each other. Brad might say, 'I've learned that I do not have to do what Dad asks the first time. I don't even have to do much when he raises his voice the first time. I do not have to do anything until he starts talking about the paddle. Then he is serious.'

Richard might be thinking that Brad is a child who just does not listen. This is partly true; but Dad is also part of the problem. If Richard would admit this, his analysis of the situation would expand: 'One thing I have learned is that my threats do not work. Anger and the paddle get results. Calm and polite requests do not. I have to do something else. I have to change the way I am handling this. I have to figure out how to get Brad to listen without always having to get out the paddle.'

Richard will have reached an important insight here. He will have realized that the way in which he reacts to Brad is part of the reason that Brad does not listen. Many parents do not like to admit this. It is easier to justify misbehaviour as a phase. Many parents cannot face the idea that they might be doing something wrong. In most situations, both you and your children need a behaviour change.

There is another lesson in this example. Whenever you use punishment alone to control a misbehaviour, you will get a re-cycling pattern of the misbehaviour. Richard threatens Brad a few times. Brad doesn't listen. Richard becomes angry and gets out the paddle. Brad becomes quiet – for a while! Sooner or later, Brad will start up again. It may be in an hour or two, or the next day, but his misbehaviour will return. Why? Because next time he may get away with it a little more than last time. Brad gets loud. Richard threatens. Brad doesn't listen. Richard gets angry. The cycle continues.

Richard needs to be consistent. He needs to follow through the first time he asks Brad to be quieter. He needs to follow Brad's refusal to play more quietly with a consequence, such as taking away the stereo or some other privilege.

Here is an example of co-operation. Mrs Harmon and eleven-year-old Jane have an agreement. For every thirty minutes that Jane studies or reads a book, she may watch thirty minutes of television. The agreement has been written down. Mrs Harmon has found no need to nag or argue with Jane. Jane clearly understands her part of the bargain. What have mother and daughter learned from this arrangement? They have learned to co-operate. Mrs Harmon has found a way to get Jane to read. Jane has found a way to earn TV time.

This type of agreement is called a contract. Children learn what you expect from them. Children learn what they can expect from you. Written contracts are useful tools for teaching responsibility, especially with teenagers. You will learn more about contracts in chapter 7.

What's the Payoff?

These examples demonstrate that parents and children learn from each other. How does the learning actually happen? In all three examples, the principles of learning are the same. Learning occurs because of a payoff. We behave to earn a payoff. We do things to get what we want. Let's examine the behaviour and the payoffs in each example.

Michael's behaviour was a tantrum. Michael's payoffs were the chocolate bar and winning over Mum – power and control. Connie's behaviours were giving in and buying the chocolate. Connie's payoffs were a few minutes of peace and no further embarrassment. They each got what they wanted. What's wrong? The method. Michael got what he wanted by screaming in public. Connie got what she wanted by giving her authority and control to her child. Michael is only four. If Michael is demanding at four, he is likely to be incorrigible at fourteen.

Brad's behaviour was ignoring Richard's requests. Brad's payoff was having his way a little longer. At first, Richard's behaviour was to threaten and do nothing. Once he was angry, Richard's behaviour was to get the paddle. His payoff was that Brad finally became quiet. The paddle has some immediate payoff, but it is not effective in the long run. Brad is not learn-ing to be quiet. He is not learning to co-operate. He is learning that he only has to become quiet when Dad brings out the pad-dle. If Brad is like most children, he will become noisy again. Dad will go through his threats again. The cycle may never end.

Jane's behaviour was spending time doing homework and reading. She has learned co-operation and self-control. Her payoff was more TV time. Mrs Harmon's behaviour was allow-ing Jane more TV time because Jane was making good decisions about homework. Mrs Harmon has learned to negotiate and plan. Mrs Harmon's payoff was that Jane is studying and read-ing more. Not only do both parent and child get what they want, the method for getting what they want is constructive rather than destructive.

How to Redirect Misbehaviour

If your child misbehaves frequently, it means that he has not learned appropriate methods of getting what he wants. Think about your child's payoff. What does your child hope to gain by this misbehaviour? Figure out the payoff and then do not give in. Do not reward unacceptable behaviour. Teach him to redirect his behaviour. Give him an appropriate alternative that will enable him to earn his payoff. If he seeks attention, show him how to get your attention without misbehaving: 'Matthew, I will not give in to you. If you want me to read you a story, you need to stop whining. Please go and sit down for few min-utes. Then come back and ask me in a polite voice.' Teach him there are acceptable ways of getting what he wants. This takes time, commitment, and planning.

Connie stopped giving in to Michael's shouted demands. She taught him how to get what he wanted through proper behaviour: if you help with the shopping, stay calm, and have a little patience, you can earn a little treat. Everyone is happy, and the mother has remained in charge of the situation, not the child.

Your Turn

Kyle has an answer for everything. No matter what Debbie asks him to do, he argues. When she says, 'Kyle, would you please take the rubbish out to the garage?' Kyle frowns and is annoyed: 'I'll do it later. Why do I have to do it now? Can't somebody else do something for a change?' Debbie is not sure what to do. She tries to explain why Kyle should do what she asks. She tries to stay calm but ends up getting angry and frustrated. When she does, Kyle gets worse. He becomes angry and hostile. He screams and yells and has a tantrum. Debbie cannot take these outbursts. After a few minutes of fighting and arguing, Debbie gives up. She takes out the rubbish herself. Kyle pouts for a few more minutes and then returns to normal. What is Kyle's payoff for arguing? What is Debbie's payoff for giving in? Write down your answers before reading further. For now, just think about the payoffs. You will read about solutions in the next chapter.

_____

_____

_____

_____

We make decisions about our behaviour to get what we want. Sometimes we want things. Sometimes we want our way. We avoid behaviour that might cause us to lose things or make us feel uncomfortable.

Kyle's payoff was getting his way. He argued to avoid doing what his mother asked. Debbie's payoff was putting an end to the battle. She got peace and quiet.

Understanding payoffs enables you to make changes in the way you discipline your children. Think about your child's payoff for misbehaviour. Does he get his way? Does he succeed in getting you angry and upset? Does he manage to avoid doing what you ask? Once you identify your child's payoff, you have your first new discipline tool. Then determine your payoff. What makes you react the way you do? Do you give in to avoid a hassle? Are you afraid of what your child might do if you do not give in?

If you want your children's behaviour to change, look at your own behaviour. This is an uncomfortable experience for me; it may also be uncomfortable for you. Try not to feel threatened or defensive, but make a commitment to change yourself first. Your change in behaviour affects your children's change in behaviour. The way that you behave towards your children affects the way they behave towards you and everyone else. There is a good title for a book somewhere in there.

Part III

How to Focus on the Positive Behaviour and Attitudes in Your Children

Chapter 5
Spotlight Good Behaviour

Joey decides to stop associating with Tim. He has decided that Tim gets into too much trouble. Joey's parents praise his decision: 'That took a lot of courage. It shows you are thinking for yourself. Growing up isn't always easy. You seem to be handling it quite well. We are proud of you. We hope you are proud of yourself.'

Tiffany runs up to her mother: 'My room is clean, Mum. Come and take a look.' Mum examines the room: 'Great job, Tiffany. You should be proud of yourself. Your room looks very neat.'

Joey's parents and Tiffany's mum are using positive feedback. They are looking for good decisions and pointing out the things their children are doing well. It is like shining a spotlight on good behaviour.

Positive feedback is the most powerful tool you have to improve your children's behaviour and self-esteem. Positive feedback is a payoff for good behaviour. Positive feedback means using praise or incentives to encourage good decision making. Positive feedback is not something new, but we often forget to use it. If you desire better behaviour from your children, increasing your awareness and use of positive feedback is essential.

How to Use Positive Feedback

You can use positive feedback in two ways – to increase desirable behaviour or decrease undesirable behaviour. Using positive feedback to strengthen a desired behaviour is easy. Simply look for a good behaviour. When it occurs, reinforce it. When your children are well behaved, reward them with a few words of praise or encouragement, a hug, or a privilege.

You would like your children to share with each other. When your children share something, reinforce the sharing. You could say, 'I like the way you are sharing.' 'I see you have decided to share your toys this morning. That's a good decision.' 'I am proud of the way you are sharing the TV. That shows you are growing up. Good for you!'

Positive feedback is simple to use. The difficult part is remembering to look for the good behaviour. Often we only see the misbehaviour in our children and take good behaviour for granted. Be proactive. Strengthen good behaviour by telling your children you appreciate it. Focus on the positive aspects of your children's behaviour. That takes practice. If you increase your use of positive feedback and make no other changes in your parenting behaviour, your children will start making better decisions.

Replacement

You can also use positive feedback to eliminate or weaken a misbehaviour. This technique works with patterns of misbehaviour, not misbehaviour that is staring you in the face. To use this technique, first determine the misbehaviour. Next, determine the opposite behaviour. Six-year-old Nathan argues and fights with his four-year-old sister, Ashley. The opposite of this misbehaviour occurs when Nathan is playing nicely and co-operating with Ashley. Praise Nathan for playing nicely – 'You are helping your sister draw. Good for you,' – and playing co-operatively will *replace* fighting. He will learn a more acceptable way of playing, and the arguing and fighting will occur less often. This is a simple but effective strategy. Use positive feedback to strengthen the opposite behaviour. The original misbehaviour will decrease.

I have been convinced of the power of positive feedback for most of my professional life. For the past twenty years, I have been working extensively with school programmes for behaviour-disordered children. These programmes would often enrol children who were unable to function in a normal school programme because of their disruptive behaviour. Many of these children were seriously emotionally disturbed, many were delinquent, and many were undisciplined. Regardless of the severity of their problems, nearly every child made improvements within the first week. People who knew these children's history were amazed. How did these children improve their behaviour so quickly? The staff piled on the positive feedback and stopped looking for negative behaviour. They looked for the positive.

Most parents see the value in using positive feedback – it is common sense – but there are some who resist the use of rewards and incentives. Whenever I face this concern, I explain how children are motivated. Many children are self-motivated to be well behaved and co-operative. This is not the case with all children. Positive feedback gives children a motivational boost. It builds self-esteem. Positive feedback encourages children to be more self-motivated.

Adults need positive feedback, too. Pay cheques are an example of positive feedback; your self-motivation would not keep you at work if you were not paid. This is how our society operates. The sooner children learn this, the better. Parents who object to using rewards must remember that their goal is to have children who make good decisions. Not all children are self-motivated to achieve this goal. Using positive feedback gets things going in the right direction; then self-motivation takes over.

Aim for Self-reward

Use positive feedback that teaches your child to value himself. Say something like, 'You made the right choice because you knew it was the correct thing to do.' It is all right for children to behave and work hard to please their parents. It is better when they behave and work hard for themselves.

> Good: 'I like the way you did that.'
> Better: 'Well done. You should be proud of your-
>   self.'

The second statement creates a sense of success and self-value. It is aimed at building self-esteem. Whenever you reward your child with an incentive, such as pocket money, be sure to add a comment that causes your child to think about doing the right thing: 'You did a wonderful job on your chores. Here's your pocket money. I hope you feel good about yourself.'

Children Believe What You Tell Them

Children act the way you expect them to act. If you tell your son that he is noisy, he will live up to that expectation. If you tell your son that he knows how to play quietly, he will live up to that expectation. When you put a T-shirt on a child that reads, 'Here Comes Trouble', you are encouraging your child to think of himself as a troublemaker. Here is what many parents say to teenagers who have messy bedrooms:

> 'I do not understand why you're so sloppy. Look at this mess. What's wrong with you? You can't even keep your cupboard tidy. Aren't you ashamed? When was the last time you made this bed? You'll never change.'

What is the parent saying? 'You are a slob. That's why your room is a mess. You will always be a slob. That's what I expect from you. I am giving up hope of any improvement.' Here is the same teenager, same bedroom, different message:

> 'You know, Zack, this is not like you. You are a neater person than this. I know you can be tidy. I know you have pride in yourself. I'm sure you can do better in the future. Don't you think so, too?'

Here is what the parent is saying: 'I trust you. I have confidence in you. You can do better. Do it for your own sake.' Your child will not make radical changes overnight, but you will be planting a healthier seed in his mind.

Be specific when you praise your children. Praise the behaviour, not your child: 'Your room looks great. It looks as if you worked hard. I hope you are proud.' Do not say, 'You are such a good boy for cleaning your room.' This has a double message. Is your son not good when his room is unkempt? Be generous with praise and encouragement, but use it wisely. Undeserved praise can lead to conceit or false confidence. Do not tell your child he has worked hard if he has not.

By praising specific behaviour, you clearly indicate correct decision making. You call attention to strengths. This gives your child confidence. He will feel capable of making good decisions.

Children need encouragement, especially children with poor self-esteem and children who lack persistence and determination. Encouragement gives children a boost of motivation. It helps them through difficult situations, helps them face fears and withstand stress, and helps them solve problems and feel successful. Encouragement provides support, trust and belief.

Tell your child that you love and value him. Accept your child for what he is, not for what he does. Show trust and confidence in your child's abilities and decisions. Recognize effort and improvement.

How to Use Encouragement

How to show trust:

'I like the way you handled that.'

'Knowing you, I am sure you will do well.'

'I think you can do it.'

'I am sure you can decide this by yourself. But if you need help, I'll be right here.'

'I would like to know your opinion about . . .'

How to show the importance of hard work:

'If you keep working, you'll probably get it.'

'Working hard pays off.'

'Hard work is not always easy, but it's always worth it.'

How to point out strengths and improvements:

'It looks as if you worked hard at . . .'

'Look at the progress you have made in . . .'

'You have really improved in . . .'

How to teach children to learn from mistakes:

'So you made a mistake. What can you do about it?'

'If you are not satisfied, what can you do?'

How to encourage responsibility:

'It's up to you.'

'If you want to.'

'You can decide that for yourself.'

'Your decision will be fine with me.'

Your Turn

Patty usually puts off doing her homework until the last possible minute. Today, she comes home from school and announces, 'I have a lot of homework. I am going to get started before dinner.' What might her mother say to spotlight this decision?

Remember Kyle and Debbie? Kyle argues about everything his mum asks him to do. Debbie often argues in return. In most cases, she gives in. Kyle wins. How can Debbie use positive feedback to help neutralize Kyle's constant arguing?

Positive feedback encourages your children to make good decisions. When Patty started her homework, she made a mature decision. It would be easy to miss what Patty is doing and say something like, 'It's about time she started growing up a little.' This would be a mistake. Do not let Patty's effort go unnoticed. 'Patty, I am glad to see you've started on your homework. You will be happy with yourself when you have finished. You will have the rest of the evening free. It seems like a good decision to me.'

Use positive feedback to reduce misbehaviour. Even children like Kyle sometimes do what they are asked without an argument. Debbie needs to look for co-operation: 'Kyle, thanks for helping me fold the laundry. I appreciate your help. I really appreciate that you didn't argue about it.' By calling attention to the times when Kyle does not argue, Debbie is emphasizing his good behaviour. This will encourage more co-operation from Kyle in the future.

Children believe what you tell them, and act the way you expect them to act. If you focus on positive qualities, you will build stronger positive qualities. Use praise and encouragement that teaches your children to value themselves.

I once saw a poster with a child looking rather discouraged. The caption read, 'When I make a mistake, no one forgets. When I do well, no one sees.' Positive feedback is easy to use, but we often forget. Retrain yourself to look for the positive qualities in your children.

Chapter 6
Never Give Away the Ice Cream

Wise parents connect special activities to good behaviour. About ten years ago, I was spending a few days with a couple who are my friends from secondary school. They have three children of various ages. One evening, we all piled into their van and went out for ice cream. Later that night, after the children had all gone to bed, we began talking about being parents. Albert asked if I had any suggestions. I said, 'Never give away the ice cream.'

I explained that at no time was any connection made between their children's behaviour that day and our trip for ice cream. Successful parents connect special events to good behaviour: 'You have had an excellent day today. Mum and I would like to take you out for some ice cream.' You can be more specific: 'I saw you sharing several times today. That's something that makes Mum and me feel fantastic. When we feel good, we feel like doing something special.'

I am not suggesting that we stuff sweets in our children's mouths whenever they are well behaved. I advise most parents to avoid sweets in favour of special activities. There are many ways to make the connection between having a good day and special events: going out for dinner, going to the cinema, or even going for a Sunday afternoon drive. What about days when behaviour has not been so good? Do not go out for ice cream on bad days.

Do not give special activities away. I have always found that teachers who are good disciplinarians use this idea instinctively. These teachers make statements such as, 'Danny, you worked hard on maths this morning. Please take this note to the office for me,' or 'Jillian, you really helped Jason with his reading. Please help me hand out these papers.' I once observed a teacher who said, 'Beth, you have been pleasant to work with this afternoon. I'd like you to stay at the end of the line and shut the lights off when we go to art class.' This clever teacher made a privilege out of being last in line.

Activity Incentives

Activity incentives are things children want to do. Playing video games, talking on the telephone and going out with friends are examples of activity reinforcers. Use activity incentives this way: first you work, then you play. Clean your room before you play video games. Do your homework before you watch television. Do not get trapped by promises like, 'I will study after the film.'

Always add an encouraging comment when your child earns an activity – 'I hope you feel good about earning extra TV time.' Emphasize feeling good about yourself, not the TV time. Enhance activities by becoming involved. Playing a game is fun. Playing a game with a parent is more fun.

Special-privilege activities can include staying up late or spending the night at a friend's home. A few years ago, we were celebrating Father's Day by going to the cinema. 'When is Brother's Day?' asked Anthony. 'There is Mother's Day and

Father's Day, why not Brother's Day?' We now have a surprise Brother's Day and Sister's Day each year. We do something special for each child.

Connect privileges to good behaviour – but be careful. Do not dangle every little activity in front of your children's noses. That will give them the wrong idea. You do not want them to think they have to be perfect. They will resent you for this and develop a poor attitude about working toward goals. Allow some fun activities to happen routinely. You also do not want them to think that every time they behave, you have to come up with a special reward. Children need to learn that good behaviour is important because it is the right thing to do.

Tangible Incentives

Tangible incentives are things children want. Examples are food, toys, CDs or money. Always accompany tangible incentives with words of thanks and encouragement. 'Here's your pocket money, Sue. You did a great job on your chores this week. Good for you.'

On page 44 is a list of incentives. This list was developed with the help of more than three thousand parents over a five-year period. Whenever I taught a class, I would ask parents to write down examples of incentives that have worked with their children. I collected their ideas and compiled this list. You can use ideas from this list to create a menu of incentives. This menu can be used with charts and contracts, which are discussed in the next chapter.

Incentives for Children Who Are Under Twelve Years Old

Hugs and kisses, praise and encouragement
Complimenting your child in front of others
Using the computer
One-to-one time with a parent
Brother's Day/Sister's Day
A special day with a parent
Surprises
Thank you notes in the lunch box
Thank you notes through the post
Having lunch at school
Books/reading a story
Posters
Science kits
Working on models, building kits
Gardening
Playing games/board games/puzzles
Magic tricks
Painting or drawing supplies
Using a calculator
Playing outside/playing catch
Sporting events
Going for a walk or a family bike ride
Going for a drive in the car
Going on a mystery trip
Sitting in the front seat
New clothes
Watching television
Using the video/renting a film
Playing video games

Using the telephone
Making popcorn
Staying up late at weekends
Spending time at a friend's house
Spending the night at a friend's house
Having a friend at the house
Having a slumber party
Making a blanket tent
Camping out in the back garden
Singing songs or playing music
Special trips
Going to a relative's house
Kite flying
Going swimming/fishing/skating/bowling
Playing miniature golf
Going to the cinema
Going to the zoo/park/museum/library
Going out to eat
Allowing child to choose the restaurant
Having a pizza delivered
Bubble baths/toys in the bath
Brushing hair
Helping prepare a meal or dessert
Helping clean up
Helping Mum or Dad with projects
Treats/ice cream
Stickers/sticker books/happy faces
Stars/points on a chart
Pocket money/savings account
Mystery jar with awards inside

Incentives for Children of Twelve and Older

(Many of the items listed on pages 44–45 will also work for this age.)

Compliments
Activities with friends/going shopping
Computer time/using the Internet
New clothes
Cosmetics/hairstyling
Snacks
Pocket money/doing work to earn money
Having a weekly goal
Projects/hobby supplies
Having a friend over for lunch/dinner
Going out with a friend for lunch/dinner
Choosing an activity for the family
Time alone/being allowed to do things alone
Staying up later than younger siblings
Music/stereo time/tapes and CDs
School materials
Pets/pet supplies
Special trips with school, church, clubs
Dances/parties/evening events/dating
Telephone time/own phone line
Skateboarding
Sporting events
Playing cards
Driving lessons/using the car/getting lifts
Working on cars/using tools
Staying out late

Concerts
Cooking
Decorating their room
Picking their own time to do chores
Going on a business trip with parent

Chapter 7
Charts and Contracts

Solidify responsibility with a chart or contract. Charts are a picture of the agreement between you and your children. A contract is a written agreement between you and your children. Charts and contracts help you focus on goals, help you keep records, and enable you to evaluate the behaviour that has improved and behaviour that needs further planning. Charts work best for children up to age twelve; older children usually prefer contracts.

A Simple Chart

A wallchart becomes a visual reminder to be consistent. Charts prompt you to look for good behaviour, provide positive interactions between you and your children, promote a healthy family climate, and encourage everyone to work together. Charts furnish both parents with an identical strategy. This increases consistency between parents.

Use a chart to reinforce good behaviour. Identify the priority behaviours you want to increase. List each behaviour on the chart. When your child behaves, put a smiley face in the box. At the end of the day, add up the number of faces. Points, ticks, plus signs or stickers work equally well. Awards on the chart are enough to satisfy some children, without other incentives, but some children need stronger incentives.

Trade smiley faces for a reward or incentive. Each smiley face could be worth a minute or two of extra story time, game time, or extra play time before going to bed. Some children like a reward each day plus a bonus activity for having a good week. Each smiley face could be worth game time at the end of the day. Then add up the smiley faces for the week. Having a friend to spend the night costs fifteen smiley faces. Be flexible. Do what works best.

Jenny's Chart

☺ = Two extra minutes of story time!

Behaviour	Mon	Tues	Wed	Thur	Fri	Sat	Sun
Shares her toys	☺ ☺	☺☺ ☺	☺☺ ☺	☺☺ ☺☺	☺☺ ☺	☺☺ ☺	☺☺ ☺☺
Listens the first time	☺☺ ☺☺	☺ ☺	☺☺ ☺	☺☺ ☺	☺☺ ☺☺	☺☺ ☺	☺☺ ☺
Daily total	6	5	6	7	7	6	7
Weekly total 44							

Always accompany an incentive with an encouraging statement. It is important to earn a reward, but it is more important to develop a sense of responsibility. Aim for self-reward: 'You had a great week. I'm glad Trina can spend the night. I hope you feel proud of yourself.'

Select behaviours that increase the chances of success. Do not load the chart with troublesome misbehaviours. Your child will perceive the chart as impossible. Choose some behaviours that are easy and fun. You can also change the behaviours. You may have a list of eight or more priority behaviours. Rotate two or three behaviours each week. This keeps things interesting.

Have a section for bonus points. Whenever your child does something extra helpful or kind, add a smiley face. When you see special effort, add a smiley face. Children respond favourably to this technique. You can use a chart to improve a child's attitude. Craig will talk politely to his sister. Each time that Craig is polite to his sister, catch him. Put a smiley face on his chart. Tell him you appreciate his politeness.

Eventually, you want your children to work for a few days or a week before receiving a reward. You want your children to learn that rewards require hard work. Begin with rewards at the end of each day, then require two days, and so on. I worked with a teacher who used charts. Her students could use points earned for good behaviour to buy activities and prizes. After a few weeks, she decided her students needed to work a little harder. She taught a lesson on inflation and raised the prices of all the prizes.

Some parents provide their children with a menu of incentives. Each incentive costs a certain number of points. Renting a video might cost 10 points. Making popcorn costs 10 points. Having a friend round costs 15 points. This technique teaches children to save and budget their points. It also teaches them that good behaviour and hard work are worth responsibility and freedom. Maintain high interest and motivation by changing the incentives. Every few weeks, add new items to the menu. For ideas of what incentives to use, look at the list at the end of chapter 6.

Develop charts for a week at a time. You may choose a five-, six-, or seven-day week. Some parents use charts only during the busy working week, while others use the chart seven days a week to provide a high level of consistency. Do what works. Some parents use laminated board and an erasable marker. That way the chart can be reused each week. Some parents draw a grid on a sheet of paper and make several photocopies. Some parents create the chart on a computer. They can make changes and print a new version each week.

Develop charts with your children. Dual participation allows children to have ownership in the chart. Let your children draw designs and colour the chart. Let them suggest some of the behaviours and incentives. Involvement creates interest and motivation.

Charts provide you with a vehicle for immediate reinforcement. You can use a chart to call attention to good behaviour. When your child behaves, walk over and add a smiley face. Charts tell your children what you expect from them and what they can expect from you. Charts encourage children to remember the rules. You can use charts to redirect a child who is beginning to misbehave:

> 'Alex, I want you to see something before you get into trouble. Look at your chart. Look how well you have been listening. Look how you have improved. I know you feel proud about yourself. I know you can make a better decision. I know you can behave.'

Here is the wrong way: 'I don't know why you can't behave for more than three days. This chart is supposed to make you behave.'

Charts help you avoid arguments. Written expectations and consequences permit no leeway for misinterpretation. Your child can see what he has or has not done. Charts teach responsibility, show your child how he is doing, and give him feedback about his behaviour. When your child is doing well, a chart shows progress. This creates feelings of success and increases motivation. When your child is not doing well, a chart will show exactly the behaviour he needs to improve. You and your child can concentrate on the behaviours that need work.

A Chart to Promote Effort in School

Some parents have used charts to improve school behaviour. If your child's teacher asks you for assistance, ask the teacher to send you a note each day. If your child has a good day, he can earn extra smiley faces. You can be more specific with school behaviour: for example, follow the school rules; finish all your work; hand your homework in on time.

Dana's Chart

★ = Three minutes of video games after homework

Behaviour	Sun	Mon	Tues	Wed	Thur	Fri	Sat
Listens the first time	★★ ★★ ★★	★★ ★★ ★★	★★ ★ ★★	★★ ★ ★★	★★ ★★ ★★	★★ ★★ ★★	★★ ★★★ ★★
Speaks politely	★★ ★★ ★★	★★ ★★★ ★★	★★ ★ ★★	★★ ★★ ★★	★★ ★★ ★★	★★ ★★ ★★	★★ ★★ ★★
Has a good day at school		★★ ★★★ ★★	★★ ★★ ★★	★★ ★ ★★	★★ ★★★ ★★	★★ ★★ ★★	
Bonus points	★★ ★★ ★★	★★ ★ ★★	★★ ★ ★★	★★ ★★ ★★	★★★ ★★ ★★★	★★★ ★★ ★★★	★★ ★★★ ★★
Daily total	18	25	21	22	27	26	20
Weekly total	18	43	64	86	113	139	159

Dana's teacher sends a note home each day. Dana can receive up to three stars a day for each of the three types of behaviour listed on his note. Ask your child's teacher to award the stars at school, and stick the stars on the chart at home.

Check-lists

A chart can be used as a check-list. Use a check-list whenever you ask your child to do a task that has several parts. Check-lists promote success by breaking a complex set of behaviours into bite-size pieces, so the task does not look so overwhelming to the child. Use a check-list for morning routine, bedtime routine, cleaning bedrooms or weekend chores.

Getting ready for bed

	Mon	Tues	Wed	Thur	Fri
Put dirty clothes away	✔				
Brush my teeth	✔				
Have my bath	✔				
Go to the toilet	✔				
Read for 20 minutes	✔				

Check-lists teach children accountability, as well as teaching them about the adult world. There are recurring events in our lives that are not always exciting and stimulating. We do these jobs to keep order in our lives. It is best to teach these responsibilities to children when they are young. A check-list may or may not earn other rewards; some parents do not think it is wise to use rewards to teach children household duties, while others do use rewards. Use what works for your children.

Contracts

A contract is a written agreement between you and your child that specifies what you expect from her and what she can expect from you. Contracts work well for teenagers. A contract can be used for the same objectives as charts: effort in school, a checklist of behaviours at home, or chores and pocket money. A contract can be very similar to a chart. I have worked with many teenagers whose contract looked like a chart in every way except that the word chart was changed to contract at the top of the page – contract sounds better. A contract can look like a chart, or it can look like a real contract.

Be specific when you write a contract. Do not say, 'Courtney will be good for two weeks.' Clarify what 'being good' actually means. Expectations that are clearly written cannot be the subject of an argument. Develop a contract for one or two weeks at a time.

A contract teaches teenagers to be responsible and gives them direction and incentive. They learn what to do and why it is important. Contracts motivate teenagers to make good choices, and help them feel mature and important.

Contract
Between Dad and Courtney

Courtney agrees to:
1. Have all her homework handed in on time.
2. Keep her room clean.
3. Help with dinner on Monday and Wednesday.
4. Clean the garage on Saturday.

At the end of two weeks, Courtney will earn a slumber party and invite three friends.

Dad agrees to:
1. Pick her friends up before seven o'clock.
2. Let the girls listen to music.
3. Buy a pizza.
4. Rent a video.

Signed _____ (Courtney)

Date _____

Signed _____ (Dad)

Date _____

Charts and contracts enable your children to plan for long-term goals. Suppose your child wants to earn a new outfit. The cost of a new outfit necessitates that your child may have to work for several weeks. Charting or contracting his behaviour and work around the house enables you and your child to monitor his progress toward his goal.

Top Ten Reasons to Use Charts and Contracts

Charts and contracts:

10. Solidify your improvement plan and provide a picture of a behavioural agreement between you and your children.

9. Enable you to focus on specific, positive, priority behaviours and attitudes.

8. Provide a written record so you can evaluate progress.

7. Act as a tangible, visual reminder to be consistent. They give both parents the same tool.

6. Promote a positive family climate. Encourage everyone to work together.

5. Can be used to redirect inappropriate behaviour and help improve poor days.

4. Encourage children to remember the rules, and teach them about accountability.

3. Create feelings of success and internal motivation, which builds self-esteem.

2. Give children immediate, positive feedback on their accomplishments.

1. Give *parents* immediate, positive feedback on their accomplishments.

Chart-making Guidelines

Create the chart with your child (ownership).

Do not overload the chart with troublesome types of behaviour.

Maintain a high level of interest by changing priority behaviours occasionally.

Provide your child with a menu of incentives. See the chart below for some examples.

Weekend Menu

Overnight friend	15 points
Making popcorn	10 points
Ordering a pizza	30 points
Renting a video	10 points
Playing miniature golf	25 points
Going out for lunch	30 points
Buying a new CD	30 points
Going to the zoo	15 points

Chapter 8
How to Use Rules and Consequences

Rules tell your children how you want them to behave. Rules are expectations, and expectations guide children's decision making. There are three factors to consider when developing expectations or rules. Expectations must be specific, reasonable and enforceable.

Expectations are specific when they communicate precisely what your child should or should not do. Most parents do not give their children clear and specific expectations. 'Clean your bedroom once a week' is not specific. A specific expectation would be:

Bedroom cleaned every Saturday morning before noon.

Checklist:
- ❏ All dirty clothes put in the laundry basket.
- ❏ All furniture dusted and polished.

❑ Carpet vacuumed.
❑ Sheets changed.
❑ All toys in toy box.
❑ All clean clothes put away.

Look at expectations from your child's point of view. 'Clean your room' can be vague and unclear. The task may look insurmountable to your child. A check-list gives your child exact steps to do – one at a time.

Expectations must be reasonable. Can your child accomplish the expectation or rule? The above check-list is specific, but it is unreasonable for a three-year-old. You can expect a young child to keep clothes and toys put away, but not dust and vacuum or change the sheets.

Expectations and rules must be enforceable. You can see when your child's bedroom is clean. The check-list is enforceable. Many parents have expectations that are not enforceable. This occurs often with teenagers. 'You may never associate with Nicole again' is not enforceable. You cannot follow your daughter around school. You cannot control all the places your daughter may associate with Nicole. It would be more enforceable to restrict Nicole from coming to your home. 'You may not invite Nicole to our home.'

A few well-developed rules and expectations are better than many poorly developed ones. Have a set of rules. Have a rule for co-operation, listening the first time, or following directions. Have a rule for morning and evening routines. Have a rule about chores. Have a rule about homework time. Rules help you be consistent. They help you focus on priority behaviours.

Consequences Teach Decision Making

Children earn positive consequences for choosing to follow rules, and negative consequences for not following rules. Consequences teach children how to make decisions; good decisions result in positive consequences, while poor decisions result in negative consequences. Consequences teach children that there is cause and effect in the world: 'This is what happens when I choose this kind of behaviour.'

Consequences must also be specific, reasonable and enforceable. A consequence is specific when the child knows exactly what is going to happen. 'If I choose this action, this will be the result.' Consequences are reasonable when they make sense. Most parents are more reasonable when they are not angry.

Consequences must be enforceable. Choose consequences that you control. A physician asked my advice. He promised his twelve-year-old 'anything he wanted' if he came top of his class. The boy came top of his class and asked for a dune buggy. I told Dad he got off too easily – the lad could have asked for a Porsche. Do not promise things you cannot deliver just to excite your child's motivation.

A mother told this story from her adolescence. Her father promised her a car if she improved in school. She remembered wondering, 'Am I so bad and lazy that my father has to offer me a car to do better?' Her father's offer was well intended, but it backfired. Promising a car was overdoing it. It made her feel worse instead of encouraging her.

'It's Your Decision'

Use rules and consequences to teach your children that behaving in a responsible manner is their choice. Their choices determine their consequences. You do not.

'Stephanie, I would like you to be home for supper every day by five o'clock. I will trust you to be on time. You have shown a lot of responsibility lately. This will be an opportunity to prove your maturity.' Mother gives Stephanie an incentive for being home on time. 'If you are home on time, you can stay up an extra half hour and go out and play the next day.' Mother also explains the punishment: 'If you choose to be late, you will go to bed at your regular time and not have playtime the next day. It's your decision.' Stephanie agrees.

When Stephanie is home on time, Mother compliments her.

If Stephanie comes home late, Mother could say, 'I'm really sorry you were late, Stephanie. It's too bad you will miss the last half hour of your favourite show tonight. I really wanted you to see it.'

Notice how this plan puts the responsibility on Stephanie, not Mum. Mum is still a nice person. She is on Stephanie's side. Stephanie makes the choice to go to bed early when she chooses to be late. Once expectations and consequences are set, stick to them. Be consistent. Be flexible before you establish expectations, not after an infraction.

Reality Consequences

You have read about tangible consequences and activity consequences in chapter 6. Reality consequences occur naturally. A child who refuses to eat dinner goes hungry. A child who refuses to wash will develop body odour. When schoolfriends begin commenting, the youngster will begin washing. Reality consequences also have positive results. A child who studies gets good grades. A child who does his chores earns pocket money. A youngster who exercises feels healthy. Reality consequences teach responsibility and decision making because they permit children to learn from the real world. Use reality consequences whenever possible.

When expectations are too difficult, children become discouraged. Do not expect perfection. When expectations are too easy, children take advantage. Expectations are appropriate when children have to put forth effort without frustration.

Behaviour is a choice. Tell your children how you expect them to behave, then follow through with appropriate consequences. Be consistent with this technique and your children will make better decisions and choose responsible behaviour.

Chapter 9
How to Be Proactive

To be proactive means to plan. Life is easier when you plan ahead. Many discipline problems can be avoided with a little planning. Planning makes use of the only advantage that we have over our children: experience. We are not more intelligent, and they have more time and certainly more energy. If you plan, you will have fewer problems.

Anticipate

Suppose you are taking your children out for pizza. You know the restaurant will be crowded. There are many video games and other expensive distractions. You want your children to have fun, but you do not want to spend all your time chasing them around. Anticipate problems. Should I let them play games before the pizza is ready? How many games should I allow them to play? How long should we stay after we finish the pizza? Think ahead. Then tell your children exactly what you expect. Lay down the ground rules before you leave the house. Let them know what happens if they do not co-operate. Let them know what happens if they do co-operate:

> 'You have had an excellent week, so we are going to Playtime Pizza for supper. You can play two video games while we are waiting for the pizza. If you listen to my directions, you can play two more games after we eat. I want you to have fun, but I also want you to behave. If you do a good job this time, I will want to take you again some day. It's up to you. We'll be leaving in ten minutes.'

Anticipate problems. You know the places where your children typically misbehave: the supermarket, church, and Grandma's house. If you suspect there might be a problem, talk with your children before you leave. Tell them what you expect from them and what they can expect from you.

Think about your child's misbehaviour. What are the recurring problems? What can you do to prevent these problems in the future? If your children argue, develop a plan to eliminate arguing. If your teenager is not motivated to do well in school, develop a plan that encourages motivation in school.

Proactive Shopping

Taking children shopping can be difficult. Children want everything they see. Shops are notorious for positioning items at child's-eye level and within reach. Teach your children that they cannot always have everything they see. When Anthony was about four, I would take him on practice trips to the toy shop. I would explain the rules before we left.

> 'Would you like to go to the toy shop?'
> 'Sure, Dad.'
> 'We are going to look and play. But we are not going to buy anything.'

'What do you mean?'
'We can go and have fun. But today is not for
   buying. Do you still want to go?'
'Yes.'

We would go and have fun at the toy shop and leave without buying anything. Anthony would often ask to buy something just to see if I remembered. I would tell him not today, maybe some other day. We would go on these practice trips about once a month. Not only was I teaching him that you cannot always buy what you want, we had a lot of fun in the process.

Planning for Improved Behaviour

The following planning guide combines many of the ideas in this book into a set of specific strategies. This is a step-by-step method of planning. Follow these steps, and behaviour will improve.

Step 1: Establish your goal. How would you like things to be? What changes do you want to see in your children? When choosing a goal, base your decision on two factors. First, select a goal that offers a high chance of success. Your first plan must be successful, as success encourages more success. Do not start with the misbehaviour that is most troublesome. Second, select a goal that contributes to the success of the whole family. This will encourage a positive family climate.

<u>Goal:</u> Danny and Allison will get along with each other.

Step 2: Make a list of specific behaviours that you want to increase or decrease. What does getting along with each other really mean? What do you expect? These are your priority behaviours.

1. Danny and Allison will argue *less*.

2. Danny and Allison will tease each other *less*.

3. Danny and Allison will share each other's toys *more*.

4. Danny and Allison will call each other names *less*.

5. Danny and Allison will co-operate *more*.

<u>Step 3</u>: Select one or two priority behaviours to change.
Choose behaviours that are easy to correct. Quick success is
important.

<u>Step 4</u>: Observe and keep a record for five days. Once you
have selected priority behaviours, count the number of times
the behaviours occur each day. Do not do anything to change
the behaviours. Simply observe them. You need to know how
often the behaviours are occurring before you carry out the rest
of the plan. This will enable you to evaluate your success.

Assume you have selected behaviours 1 and 3. Danny and
Allison will argue less. Danny and Allison will share each others' toys more. Count and record the number of times Danny
and Allison argue. Count and record the number of times they
share toys. Do this for five days. Here is a record.

Behaviour	Day 1	Day 2	Day 3	Day 4	Day 5
Argue	7	6	9	3	5
Share	1	0	2	0	0

Determine the current level of behaviour before you begin
applying consequences. This chart tells us that Danny and Allison argue an average of six times a day. They share less than
once a day.

These records are very important; they will tell you if your
plan is working. If you do not keep written records, you will be
depending on your perception and memory. With some children, improvements come slowly. Some improvements are not
easily detected. At the start of the plan, Danny and Allison are

arguing an average of six times a day. Suppose that after two weeks, they are arguing five times a day. This is a small improvement – but it is still an improvement. If left to your perceptions, you would probably say the plan is not working. You would be incorrect. You are making progress, though it is so slight that you may not see it. Written records will show any amount of progress.

Step 5: Decide how you will intervene. What will you do to change the behaviours? What reinforcers will you use? What punishments will you use? Make a list of rewards and punishments. Ask your children for their ideas when you explain the plan. What incentives would they like to earn? Use charts, contracts and menus of incentives to give your plan power.

Step 6: Explain the plan to your children. Tell them your goal. Explain the priority behaviours. Establish the rules and consequences. Clarify what you expect from them and what they can expect from you. Be positive about the plan: tell them that this is going to make everyone feel better. Tell them you are serious about the plan; you will follow through with punishments if they choose to misbehave.

> 'Children, I would like to talk to you about a new programme. I expect that from now on, you will not argue. I also expect that you will share each other's toys. When you share and do not argue, you can earn extra minutes at story time. If you break a rule, you will go to time-out for five minutes. This plan will help you behave and get along with each other. I know you can do a good job.'

From that moment, the choice to behave is with Danny and Allison. Mother can become a spectator, cheering for Danny and Allison to be winners, to be successful. When the children break a rule, Mother does not need to engage in lengthy arguments. Mother simply enforces the consequences. Mother is on their side. She is not the bad guy. Mother does not decide what happens. The children decide when they choose to behave or not.

Use plenty of encouragement. When your children show improvements, point out how well they are doing. Make comments that increase their self-worth: 'It's good to see you sharing. You should both be proud of your behaviour.'

Step 7: Evaluate. Is this plan working? Observe and keep a record as you did in step 4. By comparing these two sets of records, you will be able to determine if your plan is effective. Get your children involved in charting. Put the chart up in the kitchen. Do a new chart each week.

When your children show improvements, add another priority behaviour. Add another behaviour but maintain the originals. If there is additional improvement next week, add another. Be cautious. It is better to add new behaviours slowly. Do not rush the plan. It may collapse. If there is no improvement after three weeks, adjust the plan.

Step 8: Adjust the plan. No improvement means that the expectations are too high or the consequences are not motivating. If you think the expectations are too difficult, change them. If the children are unwilling to share each other's toys, you may change your expectation to taking turns while playing a game. Begin by playing the game with them. Model sharing and taking turns. Once they are successful, let them play a game alone. This expectation still emphasizes sharing and co-operation. As they learn to play more co-operatively, try sharing toys again.

The success of any plan depends on positive feedback and incentives. Children become tired of the same reward. Change incentives as needed to maintain a high level of motivation. See the list of incentives at the end of chapter 6 for ideas. If your children lose interest in story time, try a new incentive, such as smiley faces or stickers on a chart. Old incentives lack power.

You may be tempted to use stronger punishments if your plan shows no improvement. Stronger punishments seldom help. They discourage most children – children show less effort, not more effort. It is better to be consistent with one punishment and change the positive incentives.

When behaviours do not readily change, it is not because your child is terrible, or because you are a failure as a parent. It is because the system of expectations and consequences is not working properly.

Look at the plan. Should you make changes? Are you being consistent? Have you given the plan enough time? Are you protecting your buttons? Are consequences administered quickly? Are you giving negative attention? Are you ignoring? Are you catching your children being good? These questions will help you determine where your plan can be improved. Use the planning guide on the following pages to put your plan together.

Planning Guide

1. What behaviours do my children need to improve?

Goal: _____

2. List the specific behaviours you expect from your children.

3. Choose one or two priority behaviours to change.

4. Keep a record. Count the number of times the priority behaviours occur each day.

Behaviour	Day 1	Day 2	Day 3	Day 4	Day 5

5. What will I do?

Incentives _____

Charts _____

Contracts _____

Punishments _____

6. Explain the plan to your children. How can I get my children more involved in the plan? Outline what you want to say.

7. Evaluate. How will I know when the plan is working? Keep another record as you did in step 4. Count the number of times the priority behaviours occur each day.

Behaviour	Day 1	Day 2	Day 3	Day 4	Day 5

8. How will I adjust the plan? What other consequences can I use? Ask yourself these questions:

Am I being consistent with positive feedback?

Have I given the plan enough time to work?

Am I following through with punishment?

Am I getting angry?

Am I yelling?

Chapter 10
How to Motivate Your Children

'My son won't do anything.'
'What do you mean?'
'All he does is watch TV.'
'Does he have any responsibilities around the
    house?'
'Yes. But getting him to do them is a struggle.
    Everything is a struggle.'
'How does he do in school?'
'He passes. He could do better if he worked a little.
    He is so unmotivated.'

All children are motivated. Not all children are motivated to behave and work hard. Some children are motivated to do nothing. Think about motivation in two ways. Some motivation comes from inside you – it is internal. Some motivation comes from outside you – it is external. Being overweight is bad for your heart. Losing weight to improve your health requires internal motivation. You have a desire to lose weight. Losing weight to win a bet is an example of external motivation.

Most of us get up and go to work each day for two reasons. We get personal satisfaction from our work – internal. We also get paid – external. We need both. Most of us do not drive at a hundred miles per hour. We know it is unsafe – internal. We do not want to go to jail – external. Internal and external motivation work together to produce a responsible person.

Emphasize Success

Success creates internal motivation. When your boss praises your work, you feel successful and continue to work hard. You can use success to give your child a boost of internal motivation. Point out your child's good behaviour and decisions. Your child will feel successful. Success motivates him to work harder. When you compliment your child for having a clean bedroom, he will feel good inside – he will feel successful. He will be more motivated to keep his room clean.

Many children believe they cannot be successful. This false belief usually comes from repeated failures. Sometimes it is the result of high expectations. Correct this problem by spotlighting the positive. Point out strengths. Show your child where he has made progress. Encourage him to believe in himself. This will help your child feel success. Once success gets started, it continues. Success breeds success.

Develop expectations that build on success. This strategy is called *shaping*. When you are teaching a complex behaviour, divide the task into small sequential steps. Expect progress, not perfection. Consider this example.

Liz would like to teach Carlos how to get ready for school. This includes getting washed, brushing his teeth, getting dressed and making his bed. Liz decides that getting washed by himself has first priority. It may take a few days or a few weeks before Carlos becomes proficient at washing. Once this is accomplished, Liz teaches Carlos to brush his teeth and get dressed. Finally, Liz teaches Carlos to make his bed.

The small sequence of steps improves the probability of success. Placing all the tasks on Carlos would have been unreasonable. It may have resulted in frustration and failure. Shaping takes time. It is a good method of teaching.

Use shaping to improve behaviour gradually. Shaping means encouraging better effort. Suppose your child takes forty minutes to do a chore that should take ten minutes. Set a timer and play 'Beat the Clock.' Reinforce him for completing the job within the limit. Starting with a time limit of ten minutes may cause failure. To improve the chances for success, start with a time limit of thirty minutes. This is still an improvement over forty minutes. After a week, move the limit to twenty-five or twenty minutes. Gradually, you will achieve the ten-minute goal. Shaping improves the chance of successful behaviour.

When teaching new expectations, reinforce improvements or steps in the right direction. Do not insist on perfect performance on first attempts. Just because you have taught your five-year-old how to make his bed, do not expect him to do the job as well as you. He will be perfectly happy with a lumpy bedspread. He will steadily improve with your guidance and encouragement.

A child who misbehaves frequently lacks the internal motivation to co-operate. Use praise and encouragement to get success started. Once he experiences good behaviour, he will be more motivated to behave in the future. Tell your child when he is doing well. That will motivate him further.

Parents have a tendency to focus on negative behaviour. We tell our children what they are doing wrong. Misbehaviour gets our attention. Many parents believe that being critical of mistakes is one way to instil more effort. This is not true. Focus on what your children do well.

Your son does a mediocre job sweeping the garage. Don't say, 'You didn't sweep the corners at all. You're so lazy. A six-year-old could do better.' This type of criticism is not motivating. This is better: 'You got the middle part okay. You missed some dirt in the corners. I'll do one corner to show you how. Then you can do the rest. Do the corners as well as you did the middle, and it will look great.' This comment is encouraging. It builds success. Success motivates children to work harder.

At times, you may need incentives that are stronger than praise and encouragement. Incentives can be pocket money, toys or privileges. Use charts and contracts. Make an agreement with your child: 'Have a good week in school, and we will do something special on Saturday.' Children like working toward a goal. Do not set the standards too high. This can create too much pressure and have a reverse effect on motivation. Do not expect perfect behaviour for two months before you allow your daughter to go to the cinema. You are expecting too much.

Whenever you use incentives such as rewards or privileges, always accompany the incentive with verbal encouragement. Always remind your child that the reason to behave and work hard is to feel good about yourself. Aim for self-reward – that is always more important than the actual incentive.

> 'I hope you feel good about your week in school. You should be proud of yourself. A little hard work really pays off. I'm glad you earned the film on Saturday. But I hope you understand that the best reason to do well in school is you. Do well in school because it is good for you. You are more important than the film.'

Use Interest

Interest creates motivation. Suppose that you are trying to improve your child's reading skills. You know that your child likes dinosaurs. By reading books about dinosaurs, you will increase your child's motivation. Your child's interest in dinosaurs makes the reading meaningful and fun. Your child is motivated to learn because he is interested in what he is reading. (There is a questionnaire at the end of this chapter that will help you discover and stay in touch with your child's interests.)

Make learning interesting. With young children, you can

make changes in a child's behaviour by playing a game. Pat taught Katie how to make her bed by playing role reversal. Katie played the mum and Mum played the child. Katie liked being the mother, so making the bed became a fun-filled activity.

Family Climate

A pleasant family climate motivates children. Family climate refers to the way everyone in the family feels about each other. A pleasant family climate develops in families where members speak politely to each other and discipline is positive. Everyone feels a sense of togetherness and co-operation. Structure is balanced with flexibility. Everyone is encouraged to pursue their own interests. The family has fun together; they have inside jokes. When the climate is warm and accepting, children learn your values and goals. Children are willing to accept guidance and punishment because they see that you are acting out of love and concern. If a problem occurs, the children will rebound more quickly.

An unpleasant family climate develops in families where there is anger and criticism. The rules and structure are rigid – there is no room for individual flexibility. Everyone becomes defensive. The parents see more bad than good. The children are always picking on each other.

Family climate begins with parents who are good models. Teach your children to thank people who are nice to them, and to apologize to those they hurt. Teach them to be empathetic, and comfort others who are not doing well. The best way to teach these qualities is by living them yourself. Do not complain about helping Grandma with her shopping. Explain that helping others makes you feel good inside – that's the reward.

Make your children feel secure and safe. Children like everything in the family to run smoothly. They worry about changes: changes at school, or when Dad gets a new job. Explain changes before they happen. Reassure your children that you will always love them.

Observe other family climates the next time you go shopping. Find a place to sit and watch families. When you see a family walking together and talking nicely to one another, you are looking at a pleasant family climate. If you hear the parents say, 'Stand up straight when you walk. Hold on to that package, I don't want to lose it. Walk over here with us,' you are looking at an unpleasant family climate. If you hear the children say, 'I'm telling. You're in trouble. Tell her to stop teasing me. Look at what he is doing, Mum,' you are looking at an unpleasant family climate.

A pleasant climate can be disrupted by a negative situation, such as an argument between two children. If a situation creates an unpleasant family climate, put it behind you. Change the subject. Think of something positive. Return to a pleasant family climate as soon as possible. If two of your children have an argument, help them reach a settlement. Then redirect their energy. You may need to stay with them for a while to ensure better feelings toward each other. Go for a walk. Read a story. Get them involved in something pleasant.

A family's climate can fluctuate. Some days the climate is pleasant, other days it is not. This is normal. Aim for more good days than bad days. If one parent promotes a pleasant climate and the other does not, the children will adjust. Make your time with the children pleasant. Some pleasant family climate is better than none.

The Benefit of Humour

One important aspect of a pleasant family climate is humour. Humour can redirect the family climate. When everyone is feeling down, a little humour helps turn things around. Humour can also redirect misbehaviour. This works especially well with young children. 'Is that your Grinch face? What happened? What turned your smiley face into a Grinch face?' If your child is familiar with the story of Snow White, you can make comparisons to Grumpy and Happy.

You can also use humour for occasional forgetfulness. Your

child forgets to sweep the patio. Leave him a note: 'I hope you have a nice day on the PATIO!' You may want to tape the note to the broom handle and put it by his bedroom door. This only works well if your child has honestly forgotten. If he 'forgot' because he did not feel like sweeping the patio, humour is not appropriate. Punishment is appropriate.

Not all mischief is misbehaviour. Children can get into plenty of trouble without intending to misbehave. Mary had four young children. One day, the middle two wanted to be Mummy's helper. Mum was busy with an ill baby, so they decided to wash the kitchen floor. They had seen Mum wash the floor before. They were sure they knew what to do. One went for the mop and pail while the other went for the vinegar. They had seen mum use vinegar to clean the floors. Mary heard the commotion in the kitchen. She put the baby down. She hurried to see what was happening. When her first foot hit the kitchen floor, it slid out from under her. She slid halfway across the floor. Next to the vinegar, Mary kept the olive oil. At least, she used to.

Your Turn

Make a list of activities you can do to create and maintain a pleasant family climate. Here are some ideas to get you started:

Schedule family activities
Have dinner together.
Read stories aloud.
Develop shared hobbies.
Go to church.

Humour
Tell jokes.
Play games – have fun!
Be a little silly.

Music

Listen to each other's favourite songs.

Sing and dance.

Change of environment

Go for a walk and talk.

Go to the park.

Go out for lunch, dinner or dessert!

Write your ideas here:

_____

_____

_____

_____

Test Your Knowledge About Your Child's Interests

Knowing your child's interests helps you create motivating activities. Make two or more copies of this page. Think about one of your children. Answer each question below as though your child were answering the question. When you have finished, ask your child to answer each question. When he has finished, compare your answers to his. If your child is too young, read the questions to him – but no coaching!

1. My favourite TV show is _____.
2. What I like best about myself is _____.
3. My favourite thing to eat for supper is _____
   _____.
4. My favourite colour is _____.
5. Other kids think I am _____.
6. My favourite song is _____.
7. What I like best about my mother is _____.

8. My best school subject is _____.

9. My favourite video game is _____.

10. When I have to work around the house, I _____

_____.

11. What I like best about my father is _____

_____.

12. I like my teacher when _____.

13. My favourite film is _____.

14. I think my bedtime should be _____.

15. When I have free time, I like to _____.

16. When I grow up, I want to _____.

17. I like people who _____.

18. What I would like to change about me is _____

_____.

19. I do not like people who _____.

20. If I had lots of money, I would _____.

This exercise is not as easy as it first appears. Do not be surprised if you match only five or six answers. More than eight is great. If you want to know what motivates your children, you need to know their interests. This activity can help you understand more about your children. Repeat the activity with each of your children. You may also repeat the activity every few months. Make up your own questions. Many parents have told me that their children made a questionnaire for them. Have fun.

Family Climate Comparisons

For several years, I would ask parents who were taking my workshop to write down two or three words to describe a pleasant family climate and an unpleasant family climate. Here are the results. Remember that your goal is to keep your family's climate on the plus side as much as possible. When you have a bad climate day, put it behind you. Humour often helps.

Pleasant Family Climate	Unpleasant Family Climate
Warm	Separate
Loving	Aloof
Close	Distant
Consistent	Unpredictable
Supportive	Fearful
Understanding	Hurtful
Encouraging	Critical
Open communication	Closed communication
Admits feelings	Denies feelings
Accepting	Rejecting
Concerned	Selfish
Respectful	Hostile
Co-operative	Controlling
Quality time	Tense
Humourous	Angry
Fun	Chaotic
Happy	Sad
High self-esteem	Withdrawing
Strong	Copes poorly

Chapter 11
Self-esteem:
Motivation's Heartbeat

 Here is a teenager with poor self-esteem describing himself:

'I don't like myself much. I'm not a very popular kid. I'm not very good at sports. Who cares? My marks are average. There are a lot of things I don't want to do. I just don't understand them. I don't like trying new things; they scare me. I hate making decisions. What if I make the wrong choice? I'm not really very confident.'

Here is a teenager with healthy self-esteem.

'I'm a pretty good kid, I guess. I have a few good friends. Sometimes they listen to me. I like sports, but I'm not that great. I wish I had more time to do all the stuff I want to do. There are so many new things to learn about. Making decisions does not scare me. If I mess up, no problem. I'll figure something out to make it work.'

What Is Self-esteem?

Simply stated, your self-esteem is your attitude or belief about yourself. People with healthy self-esteem respect themselves, control their behaviour, and are confident about their decisions. Children who believe in themselves expect success from life. They feel good about themselves. They are confident. They can take constructive criticism. I have never worked with a child who was feeling good about himself and misbehaving at the same time.

People with poor self-esteem have little self-respect. They are unsure of their actions and decisions. Children with poor self-esteem have difficulty learning. They feel insecure. They lack persistence. They are oversensitive to what others think. They blame others when things go wrong.

Children with poor self-esteem see the world as a place to fear. They feel unworthy. They have low self-confidence and do not have faith in themselves. Since these children see themselves as failures, they expect failure and behave accordingly. When this happens, these children simply stop trying. For insecure children, the surest way to avoid failure and embarrassment is to avoid participation – nothing ventured, nothing failed. Not trying makes more sense than trying hard and then failing anyway. Then the child can say, 'Well, I didn't even try.' This is better than saying, 'I tried hard but failed.'

Your goal as a person should be to strive for healthier self-esteem. Your goal as a parent is to promote healthy self-esteem in your children. Give your child support and encouragement and your child will develop healthy self-esteem.

A child falls while learning to ride a bike. If you say, 'That's not how to do it. I've explained this once already. Pay attention this time,' you reduce self-esteem. Here is a more productive comment: 'Good try. You are doing better each time. I know you can do it.' This reaction shows confidence in your child's abilities. It persuades your child to believe in himself.

Extensive evidence connects poor self-esteem with drug and alcohol abuse. Teenagers place high value on what other teenagers think about them. This is natural. Adolescents with good self-esteem have a stronger sense of self-worth. They can resist peer pressure. Since they like themselves, they are less fearful of not being liked by others. Teenagers with poor self-esteem need peer approval. Since they do not like themselves very much, they need others to like them. The easiest way to get approval is to go along with the crowd. Having friends in a gang or friends who use drugs feels better than not having friends at all.

How to Develop Healthy Self-esteem in Your Children

Show your child that he is an important person by treating him with respect. The 'spilled milk' example illustrates this point. Suppose you invited your vicar to dinner. During dinner, he spills a glass of milk. How would you react? 'Accidents will happen. Don't worry, it happens all the time. Here, I'll get it. Let me clean it up.' How do you react when your child spills a glass of milk? 'Not again! I told you to be more careful. You are so clumsy. You've ruined the tablecloth.'

Accept and love your children just the way they are. This does not mean that you have to love their misbehaviour. Love your child regardless of his misbehaviour. Saying, 'I love you. I do not like what you did,' lets your child know that you love him, but you do not like his misbehaviour.

Teach your children that effort is essential to success, and persistence pays off: 'Getting a good mark for the science test will not be easy. You will have to study hard. You're clever enough to know that the hard work will be worth it. I am sure you will do just fine.' Encourage your children, and they will see that you have faith and confidence in them. Encouragement will help your children face situations with more confidence.

Do not do things for your children that they can do for themselves. Being overprotective can cause children to feel insecure or lazy. They will learn to depend on you to do things for them.

Teach your children to accept their weaknesses along with their strengths. Children with poor self-esteem only pay attention to their weaknesses. Since they dwell on their shortcomings, their positive qualities are overlooked. Explain that everyone has strong qualities and weak qualities. Use yourself as an example.

Anthony was disappointed in himself for not playing better football. I explained that each person has things they do well and things they do not do well. I used myself as an example. When I was his age, I was often disappointed. I wanted to be stronger, more co-ordinated and more athletic. Sharing my experience teaches him that it is normal to feel disappointed – but be careful. Do not say, 'I was never good at maths. You won't be either.' This will set your child up for failure.

Teach your children to overcome disappointments. Disappointments are part of life; we all have them. Teach children to experience their disappointments without the results being tragic.

Todd was seventeen. He lived day to day without much purpose until he met Michelle. They fell in love. Todd was awestruck – someone loved him. He invested his whole life in Michelle, loving her to the exclusion of all else. She was his sole reason to live. He spent every minute thinking of her. Then she dumped him, and his life became meaningless. He could not put the pieces of his life together. Todd escaped into drugs for two years. He suffered. He was alone. One day he realized he was killing himself. He got help, and he survived.

Whenever you entrust your feelings of self-worth to someone else, you risk being hurt. Your self-esteem must have roots deep within yourself. It's wonderful to feel loved – that cannot be denied – but teach your children that it is important to love and support yourself, to be your own best friend. Teach children to appreciate reasons for life – reasons for relationships, reasons to go to school, reasons to work. Teach them alternatives. If one reason fails, tragedy will not result.

Scott, a junior in secondary school, lived to play football. He was a good player – college material, maybe professional – and very popular. He hung out with the jocks and cheerleaders. He was invited to all the important parties. Then he was injured. No football for the rest of his life, no practices, no football buddies, no cheers, no glory after the victories, no reason to go to school, no reason to live.

Scott had all his self-esteem in one basket. When that was taken away he had no other way to feel good about himself. There was no purpose without football. He tried to kill himself but failed. Then he got help. It took Scott a year of therapy to see any value in his life. Scott was lucky.

You must take an active role in building your children's self-esteem. Provide encouragement and support. Give your children positive feedback whenever possible. Tell your children that they have the power to behave. Believe in your children and they will learn to believe in themselves – the best motivation there is.

Chapter 12

Being Consistent Can Make You Feel Dreadful

One evening, the four of us went out for dinner. Leah was three years old. The children knew that after dinner we often have dessert. Leah ordered her usual cheeseburger and chips and small milk with one straw. For whatever reason, Leah wanted to look around the restaurant more than eat. We gave her the familiar reminders. With each reminder, she took another nibble of her burger or sip of her milk. She was not eating very well. Meanwhile, the rest of us had nearly finished.

Realizing that she was not hungry, I wanted to be reasonable. I cut the remainder of her burger in half. 'You have to eat this half of your burger before it's time for dessert. If you do not eat, you will not get ice cream.' Leah smiled and agreed but continued to look around and not eat. Soon, the time of reckoning was upon us. It was time to order dessert.

We thought about buying her some ice cream anyway – although she had not eaten, she was polite and well behaved. We thought about the scene she would create when she found out she would not get any ice cream, and embarrassed we would be. Many parents think this way. This is how we justify giving in, especially in public. Do not give in to these thoughts.

Our only alternative was to follow through. If you do not eat – no dessert. Consistency is more important than a few tears and some embarrassment. Our choice was not what to do but how to do it. We decided that Mum and Anthony would get three ice-cream cones and meet me at the checkout counter. I would remain at the table and give Leah more time to eat, not because she could still get ice cream – it was too late for that – but because I wanted her to eat more of her dinner. The deadline for getting ice cream had expired.

After a few more minutes, I told Leah we were leaving. She asked if she could have her ice cream now. I said, 'No, you did not finish your dinner.' 'I'll eat it now, Daddy,' she pleaded. Then she saw three ice-cream cones, not four. We softly explained that we had finished our dinners, and that's why we each had ice cream.

As I carried my screaming daughter under my arm past a crowded dining room of families, I felt dreadful. I wondered what they were thinking. I wanted to explain, 'It's okay, I'm just being consistent.'

Leah cried and pleaded all the way home. She said she would eat her dinner if we would only give her another chance. All this sadness while three of us were choking on our ice cream. Anthony wanted to give her some of his. It was the first time in my life I did not enjoy eating ice cream. I wanted to roll down my window and toss it out. We love Leah. Watching her cry was excruciating.

Think About the Future

Sometimes, saying no and being consistent is not easy. It can hurt. It would have been much easier to give in and buy the ice cream. We did not. We knew it was more important to be consistent, even though being consistent is sometimes painful.

We wanted Leah to learn that Mum and Dad mean what they say, even if it means some temporary unpleasantness. You have to eat your dinner if you want dessert. If you do not finish your dinner, you will not keep the rest of us from having dessert. You have to do what you are asked, even in a public place.

About two weeks later we returned to the same restaurant. We wanted to see if our struggle had any effect. Leah ate with purpose. Occasionally, she would pause and say, 'I'm gonna eat all my cheeseburger tonight.' When the waitress delivered her ice cream, it was a double treat. Leah was happy and proud of herself. We knew that our painful experience had paid off.

Do not let little misbehaviours slide. They grow into larger problems. When we followed through with Leah, we were thinking about the future more than the present. We wanted Leah to know that she had to eat her dinner not just this time but every time.

What Happens When You Do Not Follow Through

Anna's ten-year-old son, Joel, played outside each day after school. When Joel came inside for dinner he was supposed to wash his hands before coming to the table. Every day, Joel came to the table without washing his hands. Anna would say, 'Please go and wash your hands.' Joel would go and wash his hands. He never argued about it. He was always co-operative once Anna reminded him. This went on for weeks. Joel came to the table with dirty hands. Anna would send him to wash. One day, Anna confronted Joel: 'Every day you come to the table without washing your hands, and every day I send you to the bathroom. Can you explain why you don't wash your hands first?' Joel immediately looked up at his mum, and replied, 'One day you didn't catch me.'

'One day you didn't catch me.' It may have been six weeks ago, but he got away with it one time. One time he was able to eat dinner without washing – without being caught. What a thrill! This story shows how children think, how their clever minds work. It made more sense to come to the table and be sent away than wash his hands the first time around. Why? Because he got away with it one time. One slip, and Joel tests Anna for weeks, just to see if she will slip again. That is why consistency is so important.

This story reminds me of Las Vegas. People put coin after coin into the slot machines. The occasional payoff is worth the gamble. Coming to the table with dirty hands was a gamble worth taking.

Most parents are not consistent. We say things we don't mean. We say no and then give in. We don't follow through. With a little bad behaviour, most of us change no to yes. Some days we let misbehaviours slide, others we play warden.

The Difference Between Threats and Warnings

Threats are not punishments. A threat is an *intention* to punish – a big difference. Threats are just words. Many parents threaten because they do not know how to use punishment; some threaten because they are afraid to use punishment; and some threaten because they are too lazy to follow through with a punishment. Whatever the reason, threats often make a child's misbehaviour worse.

Have you ever been in a waiting room where there were parents and young children? Mum says, 'If you do not sit down, I will put you in the car.' The child sits for a minute or two and then starts jumping around again. Mum threatens. The child sits for a few more minutes and then gets up. Mum threatens again – and so on.

Threats teach your children not to believe what you say. Children know that threats are not always enforced. How do they know? You have not persisted in the past. You have not followed through. Threatening is just a magnified form of inconsistency.

Warnings are a little different. Warnings can be effective if you use them sparingly and with plenty of judgment. Most children do not need warnings; most children know what is proper behaviour and what is not. Use a warning only when your child does not know that he is behaving inappropriately: 'Ben! That is not acceptable. Please stop.'

Not all parents can use warnings successfully. Only parents who have a reputation for following through can use warnings. Parents often ask what the difference is between a threat and a warning. The distinction is found not in what the parent says but in what your child hears.

Melody brought four-year-old David to our house for a birthday party. Midway through the party, David began to act up. Melody warned him to stop. He did not. Melody told him that they would leave the party. He continued to misbehave. She picked him up and headed for the car. He cried and pleaded to stay. They left and did not return. The party was over for David. Even though Melody also had to leave, she followed through. David has been good at parties ever since.

If you have consistently followed through with what you say, your child will hear a warning. Your child has learned that when you say stop, you mean stop now. If you have been inconsistent, your child will only hear a threat when you say stop. Your child has learned that it takes several threats before he actually has to stop.

Another type of warning can be used effectively: a time warning. Time warnings are very helpful for parents and children. Here are some examples.

'Dinner will be ready in ten minutes. Please finish your game and wash your hands by then.'

'You can play until the timer goes off. I'll set it for fifteen minutes.'

'Mum's taxi leaves in seven minutes. All aboard
by then!'

Time warnings let your children know ahead of time that something is expected of them very soon. This is less of a surprise
and generally encourages them to be more co-operative. I am
not sure why, but for some reason, children love timers. You
can use the timer on the oven, a bell timer or an egg timer. The
feedback I have received from parents confirms my belief
in time warnings and timers. Most parents have found these
techniques to be very helpful.

'Five More Minutes', 'Maybe', and 'We'll See'

Many parents are afraid to say no. Some parents do not say no
because they want to avoid an argument; some feel embarrassed
or guilty if their child has a tantrum; some are afraid of being
disliked by their children; and some are lazy and do not want to
take firm action. So parents use stall statements. Most of us
learn stall statements from our parents. 'Five more minutes',
'Maybe' and 'We'll see', three favourite stall statements, are
among the most commonly used words.

'It's time to go home.'
'Can't we stay a little while longer?'
'Okay, five more minutes.'

'Can we have some ice cream after supper?'
'Maybe.'

'Can we go to the park tomorrow, Dad?'
'We'll see.'

Stall statements delay the inevitable. It is okay to use delays
as long as your children know that 'Maybe' sometimes means

yes and sometimes means no. Your children must realize that 'We'll see' sometimes means yes and sometimes means no. Your children must understand that 'Five more minutes' means five more minutes, not ten more minutes.

Using stall statements occasionally is harmless. Use them too often and your children will whine and plead and beg, hoping you will give in. Use them carefully.

How do you teach your children that maybe sometimes means no? Every now and then, follow a maybe with a no. 'I know I said maybe. I have thought about it. The answer is no.' You may find that your children will not like hearing this. That's all right – they will live. Be consistent. It will be worth it in the long run.

What Consistency Means to Your Children

If you want self-disciplined children you need to be consistent. You need to mean what you say. You need to follow through. You can significantly improve your children's behaviour by being more positive and more consistent. All parents need to be more consistent. Consistency is the most important element in your relationship with your children, yet it is the most frequently omitted. If you change one thing about the way you discipline your children, be more consistent.

Corrine was not a strong disciplinarian. Her fourteen-year-old daughter, Joanne, behaved any way she pleased. Joanne would stay up past midnight, watching TV and talking on the telephone. She was always late for school, refused to do housework and argued about everything. Joanne ruled the home. Joanne always got her way; Corrine always gave in. Corrine and I had several meetings. We talked about consistency and follow-through. We developed a plan that gave Corrine authority. Corrine learned to follow through with mild restrictions whenever Joanne misbehaved. Gradually, Corrine saw some improvements. I asked Corrine to bring Joanne to our next session. I asked Joanne how things were going at home. She responded with a glare. 'Horrible since my mother started talking to you.' I couldn't help but smile.

Consistency means follow-through. Manage a misbehaviour exactly the same way every time it occurs. This is especially true when working with persistent misbehaviour. Once you tell your daughter to be home at five o'clock, follow through if she is late. Some parents justify being a little late to avoid a conflict – 'It's not that big a problem.' 'I'm too tired to deal with this now.' You are fooling yourself. How big must the problem be in order for you to act? Will you be less tired tomorrow?

You set the speed limit. Motorway drivers know that the true speed limit is higher than 70. Most police do not give tickets until you are travelling well over 70. If you can drive well over 70 without penalty, you will. This is the same for children. If you set the speed limit at 70, follow through at 71. If you give a little leeway, they will push for more.

When you are consistent with one child, other children learn by observing. During my first summer working at a home for boys, I was taking a van full of children on a weekend camping trip. After a few miles of travel, Lamont started getting restless. I gave him a warning. About fifty miles from home, he began teasing and instigating. I gave him another warning. He was getting worse. I told him that if he did not stop, I would turn the van around and take him back home. He did not believe me. He did not think I would follow through, and he did not stop. I did. I turned the van around. What a shock! First, he stopped misbehaving. Then he started pleading with me that he would be good. 'Too late', I said. Home he went.

It took about two hours to take Lamont home and then return to the place where I had turned around. Those were two of the best hours I ever spent. My reputation with Lamont and all the other children was made that day. Not only did the rest of the trip go smoothly, but for the next six years the story was handed down from child to child. 'You better believe what Mr Sal tells you. He means it.'

I have often wondered what would have happened if I had not turned around. Lamont would have continued to misbehave. The other children would have seen that I give threats but do not follow through. They would have started testing me.

The weekend would have been a disaster for all of us, particularly for me.

When a child misbehaves, deal with it now. If you let it slide, you will pay the price in the future. Do not let friends, neighbours or grandparents influence your commitment to be consistent – 'Let it go this time.' 'How often do we get to see him?' 'He's okay. He's just a little excited.' You are the parent, so do what is best for your children and let other people raise their own. Be consistent. Children love to get away with bad behaviour; it is your job to see that they do not.

Children learn to make decisions by predicting the consequences of their actions. Children learn self-discipline by predicting the outcome of their behaviour. They must be able to see the cause-and-effect relationship between how they behave and what happens to them: 'If I choose this behaviour, then this consequence will happen.'

Your children must be able to predict your reaction to their behaviour. They need to know how you behave. They need to know the consequences. Children will learn this cause-and-effect relationship more quickly when you behave consistently.

Consistency Between Parents

Becky was two. Her mother and father were sitting on the couch. Becky asked Mum for some yoghurt. Mum said 'No, it is too close to dinner.' Without a moment's hesitation, Becky turned to Dad and asked him for some yoghurt. Children learn to manipulate at a young age – if one parent says no, try the other. It gets worse as they grow older.

Consistency is important between parent and child, but it is also important between parent and parent. If Dad is too easy and Mum too strict, your children will quickly learn to manipulate. If your speed limit is 40 and Dad's is 65, your children will learn to take advantage. This is disastrous. Children will learn which parent to ask for what things. When you want a treat, more TV time, or a couple of extra pounds, ask Dad. He usually gives in on these matters. When you want to postpone doing a chore or have a friend spend the night, ask Mum. She's more easy-going.

Agree on the house rules and expectations. Agree on what children earn and do not earn, how and when to use punishment, and on things that relate to discipline. If you disagree on a particular rule, that's fine, but disagree behind closed doors. Work things out when your children are not around. Even if you do not agree, present a united front to your children. Compromise if you must. If you disagree in front of your children, you will be teaching them where you are vulnerable. Then you will hear statements such as, 'Well, Dad thinks it's okay,' or 'Mum said I could go.'

Talk with your spouse about discipline. Explore each other's feelings and beliefs. Review your ideas periodically. Make a list of misbehaviours. Have a strategy that deals with each misbehaviour. That way, whichever parent is around, misbehaviour will be handled consistently. When unplanned situations occur, wait for your spouse. Simply say, 'I'll have to talk with your father before making a decision. You will have to wait.' Children learn that you mean business with this approach. They will learn that you are working together. They will not be tempted to play one of you against the other.

Do not confuse this suggestion with 'Wait until your father gets home.' Do not depend on one parent to make all the decisions about discipline. Only special problems need to be discussed. Day-to-day discipline must be handled immediately. If Mum depends on Dad to be the heavy, the children will seldom listen to Mum. Mum must take charge of her time with the children.

Consistency is not always easy but it is always worth it. Think of the future: do not let little problems grow, but deal with misbehaviour immediately. Do not be afraid to say no. Talk with your spouse about discipline, even if you are divorced. Plan to manage misbehaviours consistently.

Chapter 13
How to Be More Consistent

Mrs Ellis and her five children moved into a school district where I worked. Within the first week, each child had been sent to the principal at least once. I asked Mrs Ellis to meet with me. She agreed. I began to give her my pep talk on consistency. She interrupted. 'I know I need to be consistent', she said. 'Right now I am tired. I need a little vacation from consistency.'

She had five children who needed consistent follow-through. It took a lot out of her to be consistent. Every now and then, she let go. She gave up – not completely, just temporarily. That was the problem.

You cannot be consistent some of the time. You must be consistent all the time. That is not easy: it is exhausting, it drains your energy, it weakens your spirit. Here are seven strategies that will help you be more consistent.

Emphasize Priority Behaviours

The first strategy that will help you be more consistent is the idea of priority behaviour. A priority behaviour is a behaviour that you are going to manage with special diligence and focus. A priority behaviour can be positive. If you want your children to co-operate with each other, co-operation is the priority behaviour, so focus on co-operation. Catch your children co-operating and praise them. This will teach your children that you value co-operation.

A priority behaviour can be a misbehaviour. Many children develop misbehaviour patterns. They display the same misbehaviour – such as arguing, whining, or disobeying – repeatedly. Your child may exhibit several misbehaviour patterns. Attempting to work on all of them at once would be impossible for you and confusing for your child, so choose one or two patterns as priority misbehaviours. Be aware of these misbehaviours at all times. Never give in. Do not reward them. Be consistent. This will not be easy. There will be times when you are tired and will not want to follow through. If you do not, you will pay for it later.

Priority behaviours help you focus. It is difficult to be consistent with every misbehaviour. Identify one or two priority behaviours and focus your energy on them. Be consistent and diligent with priority behaviours. Your children will learn to behave more quickly.

Remember to be positive. Every misbehaviour has an opposite, positive behaviour. Watch for positive behaviours while you are consistent with priority misbehaviours. Suppose your child's priority misbehaviour is having tantrums. Be consistent and never reward the priority misbehaviour. Never reward any tantrum. You must also reinforce your child for not having tantrums: 'I'm glad to see that you did not cry when I told you that you could not have a chocolate bar. I really appreciate that. Thank you.'

When you are consistent with priority behaviours, it will have a positive effect on all other behaviours. Your children will generalize what they learn from one situation to another. It is like having a two-for-one sale on good behaviour: be consistent with priority behaviours and get improvement in other behaviours free. How could you refuse such a deal?

Give Yourself Tangible Reminders

Using tangible reminders is the second strategy that helps you be more consistent. Write little notes to yourself: 'Do not give in to tantrums,' 'Catch your children playing quietly.' Put a sign on your bathroom mirror: 'Look for co-operation.' Put a sign on the refrigerator: 'Stay calm. Do not argue.' Notes and signs help you remember to be consistent. They help you remember to focus on priority behaviours.

I learned this in my first year teaching. Kenny and Aaron were my two top students. Handsome, articulate leaders, thirteen years old, they were very much alike. That was their problem. They hated each other and were on each other's case constantly. I tried being positive, but I was not consistent enough. It was too hard; I had tunnel vision, and could only see the bad behaviour. I had to do something. I decided to put a sign at the back of my classroom.

Catch Kenny and Aaron
being pleasant to each other!!

It was like magic. The sign was not to remind Kenny and Aaron to be pleasant to each other but to help me be consistent and positive. It helped me focus on a positive behaviour. The class thought it was a stupid idea at first, but by the end of the week every student in my class wanted their own sign on the wall. They loved all the attention. I loved all the co-operation and good behaviour.

Practise Patience

The third strategy that you need to be more consistent is patience. Parents want quick changes – children do not. Children do not change bad behaviour patterns easily. Misbehaviours that have been mastered take time to give up. Just because you decide to be consistent, your child's misbehaviour will not change overnight. You will have to be patient.

Patience is difficult – you want immediate results for your energy and commitment – but think about things from your child's point of view. If you have been using threats and warnings before taking action, your child has learned that this is how you behave. Now, you have changed. You are following through. Your child will be confused and resist change – 'I don't understand, Dad. You always yell three or four times before you really mean it.' It takes time and energy to change your behaviour, and your child is no different. Be patient.

Choose a Good Time

If you are going to initiate a new plan or start a new discipline technique with your children, choose a good time to begin. An experienced mum gave me this idea. A tax accountant, she was taking my parenting class during the early spring. She explained that she had learned never to start anything new during the tax season. She was working sixty-plus hours per week, and was not at her best at home. She recognized that this period was not a good time to make any new resolutions, start a diet, change a bad habit, or try to enforce a new behaviour with her children. Very clever, I thought.

Do not try to initiate changes in troublesome behaviour just before Christmas or the annual visit from grandparents. Choose a time that is more stable and predictable. This will give you the time and structure that you need to be consistent.

Be Mindful of the Time of Day

There are three blocks of time each day that correlate to increases in misbehaviour. Morning routine is often difficult because of pressure to be out of the door and off to work and school, which makes parents and children feel tense and urgent. This is a time when tempers erupt and reason and calm abandon us. Prepare for this each day. It is better to wake everyone up twenty minutes earlier to ensure enough time to get ready. Take ten minutes to have breakfast together and have fun. Relax. Model calmness. This teaches children to get their moods ready for the day.

Research has shown that the most difficult time of day for parents and children is the time from after school to dinner. Parents are tired. The children want to release energy that has been stored all day at school. Studies have shown that this is also a time when everyone's blood sugar is low, which makes us irritable. It may be helpful for you and the children to have a snack. It also helps to have a plan for the children. Keep them busy.

Bedtime is a problem for some children. Do not teach your children that going to bed is a punishment that comes at the end of each day. Going to bed is a time to relax and get comfortable. Have a bedtime routine: bath, snack, story, hug and kiss. Use a chart or checklist to teach children to regulate their own bedtime routine. Do not use going to bed early as a punishment. Being sensitive to these difficult times of day helps you focus and be more consistent.

Expect Challenge

Children will test you. No matter how carefully you plan or how strongly committed you are, your children will resist change. Children often respond well to new discipline techniques at first, but after a while, they drift back to previous patterns, and misbehaviours increase. When this happens, do not despair; this is normal. Once you realize that occasional testing of limits will occur, you will be less frustrated and disappointed. Knowing this will help you be more consistent during these periods.

Make the Commitment

The seventh strategy that helps you be more consistent is the awareness that consistency is one of the most important factors in successful parenting. Consistency teaches children what to expect. It teaches children how to predict the consequences of their actions. Once a child can predict the outcome of his behaviour, he will make better choices. Making better choices is the key to developing responsibility.

Understanding the importance of consistency will make you more consistent. Consistency is important when teaching positive behaviours. The more consistently you use positive feedback, the more quickly your child will learn appropriate behaviour. This is especially true when you are trying to teach new priority behaviours. Every time you find your children playing nicely, thank them for being co-operative. When you see your son making an effort to clean his room, mention how proud you feel. Explain how he is growing up and becoming responsible, as well as helping the whole family.

Consistency is important when you use punishment. Once you tell your child that a misbehaviour will be punished, always follow through. If you slip up or use punishment only when you feel like it, you will make the problem worse. You will teach your child that you do not mean what you say. You will teach your child to be persistent in a negative way; sooner or later, he will get away with misbehaving.

Consistency is an expression of love and caring. When you behave consistently, your children will have better self-discipline. They will see that they are important to you: 'I know my parents care about me because they put in the energy and time to make sure that I behave.' When you behave consistently, you are telling your children that you will do whatever it takes.

That's your job. Children seldom verbalize that they prefer parents who follow through, but they do. It is especially important to teenagers.

Inconsistency causes children to be unsure of themselves. It makes children feel unimportant, insecure and confused. This confusion compels children to manipulate, whine, or take advantage of unclear situations. Once your children learn that you mean what you say and are consistent, they will take you more seriously and think more carefully about all their behaviours and decisions. Thinking is what you want.

The next time that you feel you need a holiday from consistency, remember Mrs Ellis. Think about the consequences. Misbehaviour will get worse, and will happen more frequently. Inconsistency teaches children that you do not mean what you say. Once your child learns this, he will try to get away with other misbehaviour: 'If I can get away with skipping my chores, let's see what happens when I come home late.' Consistency breaks this cycle.

A certain amount of misbehaviour is normal in all children. When you respond to misbehaviour consistently, the misbehaviour will decrease. When you respond to misbehaviour inconsistently, the misbehaviour will increase.

Part IV
How to Manage Misbehaviour

Chapter 14
How Children Learn to Misbehave

'Please do the dishes, Paul.'
'I don't feel like it now.'
'Paul, it's your turn to do the dishes.'
'Can't I do them later?'
'It's time now, Paul, please.'
'I don't want to do the dishes tonight.'
'Do the dishes, and I'll give you a pound.'
'Make it two pounds, and you've got a deal.'

This parent is offering a reward to a child who is arguing and trying to avoid doing his job. *A bribe is a reward for misbehaviour.* A bribe is an attempt to coax a misbehaving child into good behaviour.

Bribery makes children obnoxious. Bribery places power in the hands of your children. Do not use bribes to persuade your child to change his mind. When you bribe a child, you are encouraging him to be disagreeable in the future: he will think,

'I refused to do the dishes. Now I am two pounds richer.' If a child misbehaves, deal with it. Do not be tempted by bribery.

When Michael had a tantrum in the supermarket, Connie bribed him into being quiet by giving him a chocolate bar. She rewarded him for badgering and whining. Although she got a quiet child, Connie will now get a tantrum every time she takes Michael shopping; Michael has learned that *tantrums get him what he wants.* This is the way patterns of misbehaviour develop.

Many reasonable and well-meaning parents have accidentally or unintentionally taught their children to misbehave. Connie never intended to teach Michael to have tantrums. If you were to ask her if she was teaching Michael to misbehave, she would be appalled: 'Are you joking? I have worked my head off trying to get him to behave.'

Some parents begin rewarding unacceptable behaviour while their children are quite young. Consider the parent who uses a treat to comfort an unhappy child. The treat will probably coax the child into a better mood, but the youngster may also learn that one way to get a treat is to act unhappy, and will associate unhappiness with food. Whenever something unpleasant occurs, food will make the hurt go away.

Some circumstances in life are unpleasant. We need to face these events without a sweet on our lips. This connection between food and discomfort in childhood often results in poor eating habits in adulthood. Think about sitting around the house with nothing to do. How many times do you look in the refrigerator?

Whining, Badgering, and Tantrums

Children whine, badger, and have tantrums to get their way. Children are experts at manipulating their parents. Some of this comes naturally; some we teach them. Giving in to tantrums and other demands causes misbehaviour to increase in the future. Often we establish this pattern by the time a child is two years old.

Almost every time you go shopping, you see a child like Michael. You may have been humbled yourself a few times. I have been. Before I became a parent, I used to wonder how children got away with this. Now it's clear. It's easy to give in.

When a child gets what he wants by having an outburst, he learns there is a payoff for misbehaving. Once learned, this pattern is difficult to change. You change it by not giving in. Stop the payoff.

Extinction

Behaviour that is not rewarded will not recur. This is called *extinction.* Behaviours that are not paid off will stop happening. For extinction, you must eliminate rewards that follow a child's misbehaviour. You must eliminate the payoffs that encourage more misbehaviour in the future. Extinction means that Connie must stop giving Michael a chocolate bar, no matter how embarrassing his tantrum becomes.

With parental persistence and consistency, tantrums and demands that are not rewarded will eventually disappear – but the key word is *eventually.* Behaviour change takes time. (Remember reading about patience in chapter 1?) In many cases, tantrums will get worse before they get better. Consider the child's point of view: 'I usually get what I want by having a tantrum. Now Mum is ignoring my tantrums. I'll get her attention this time. I'll show her a tantrum she will never forget.' It is not at all uncommon for tantrums and demanding misbehaviour to intensify for a brief period when you stop giving in to them. This increase is called an *extinction burst.* Children who are persistent have greater tantrums at first. The more a child has been rewarded, the more the misbehaviour will resist extinction.

Once you decide to stop giving in, you must do so forever. Never give in again. Imagine what would happen. Connie decides that she will not give in to Michael's tantrum. She will not buy him the chocolate he demands. Off they go to the supermarket. By aisle 3, Michael is having a tantrum. Connie hangs in there. Michael's face is getting red. So is Connie's. Aisle 5 – they have never made it this far without the chocolate. Michael is yelling and screaming and kicking. The situation has never been this bad. Connie's knees are getting weak. So is her will. Aisle 7 – Michael is in a frenzy. Connie holds out and holds out and holds out. As Michael is about to launch a jar of raspberry preserves at an astonished bystander, Connie's will crumbles. She gives in. Everyone is calm as Michael eats his chocolate bar quietly in aisle 9.

Connie has just taught Michael to have bigger tantrums and be more persistent. Once you decide to stop giving in, you must do so always – even when you are tired, even when you do not feel like being consistent, even when you have had a long, miserable day. If you start to use extinction and then give in, you will make the misbehaviour worse. If you give in to bigger tantrums and demands, you will be rewarding bigger tantrums and demands. You will get longer and louder tantrums in the future.

Be consistent. Follow through. Once you say it, do it. If you do not think you can outlast the extinction burst, then do not start. Wait until you have the courage and the energy. You will need support from your spouse. It is important to work together; it will emphasize the point to your child that you both mean business. If your spouse will not co-operate, be consistent anyway. It will take a little longer for your efforts to show results, but your child will learn that you mean what you say, and he will behave better for you. He will behave as always for your spouse.

Be patient. Most parents fail because they lack patience. You must be more persistent than your child. If you give in, you lose. You must control yourself. Do not yell or lose your temper; that will only make matters worse. Your reward will be well-behaved children.

If you have a bad day, put it behind you. If you give in, do not dwell on it. If you are short on patience, regain your balance. Being patient and consistent is not easy. If you slip back into old habits, do not criticize yourself. Start fresh. Think of the future.

You Cannot Eliminate Some Payoffs

Extinction weakens misbehaviour that is demanding or attention-getting. Extinction will not improve all misbehaviour; there are some rewards for misbehaviour that you cannot eliminate. Consider the teenager who smokes cigarettes. You can forbid smoking in the house, throw away the cigarettes when you find them, and even punish the youngster. These sanctions may help curtail the smoking, but there are payoffs that you cannot control. You cannot control peer pressure: his friends encourage smoking, he earns social status by smoking, smoking is what everyone else is doing. Since you cannot eliminate all the rewards for smoking, despite your efforts, smoking will continue.

Extinction Works Both Ways

Extinction weakens misbehaviour, but it also weakens good behaviour that is not reinforced. When positive behaviour is ignored, it may be replaced by misbehaviour. Your child will think, 'Why be good? It's not worth it.' Use positive feedback when your children are behaving. Do not ignore good behaviour; focus on what your children are doing right. Catch your children being good.

Do Not Make Excuses

Some children misbehave because parents make excuses – 'He's just tired,' 'She's had a long day,' 'He hasn't eaten,' 'She always acts that way when he is around.' Sometimes we teach our children to misbehave by making excuses for them.

When you make excuses, you are implying that your child is not capable of behaving. Excuses teach children they do not have to be responsible for their behaviour; misbehaviour is justified as long as you can come up with a good reason. Making excuses will come back to haunt you. When you make excuses, you are giving your children reasons to misbehave in the future. They will use these excuses to argue and avoid responsibility.

Many teenagers were taught to be irresponsible by their parents. When these teenagers were younger and still impressionable, their parents made excuses for them.

Never Ask Why

One way to avoid buying into excuses and teach responsibility at the same time is to avoid asking why. The question Why? asks for an excuse. The question What? does not. Rather than ask why, ask what. Asking why usually leads to long arguments or debates. Asking what helps your child focus on the misbehaviour. Here is how this works. Instead of asking a question such as, 'Why did you do that?' ask your child 'What did you do?' The purpose of asking the 'what' question is to avoid the excuses and have your child simply tell you what happened. Some children resist this at first. They are in the habit of answering 'why' questions. Do not let them tell you why they did it. You need to help the youngster describe what he did. So if your child tries to tell you why he did it, stop him. Say, 'I didn't ask you why you did it. I asked you to tell me what you did.' Once you get your child to describe what he did, talk about correct behaviour. 'What could you have done so you would not be in trouble now?' This approach avoids making excuses. (See chapter 22 for more about this strategy.)

We are tempted to bribe children into behaving because there is a temporary payoff and we like quick solutions. But bribery teaches children to be more argumentative and oppositional.

It encourages more misbehaviour. Do not reward unacceptable behaviour. Do not give in to demands, whining or badgering. Stop the payoff permanently. Be consistent and patient.

Do not make excuses. When a child misbehaves, deal with it – always. Excuses give children reasons to misbehave.

Chapter 15
Why Children Push Your Buttons

It's 10:10 and thirteen-year-old Megan is still on the telephone. The rule is, there will be no telephone conversations after ten o'clock. Mother sticks her head into Megan's room and politely reminds her that she needs to finish the conversation and hang up. Megan nods and makes a face. At 10:20, Mother calmly reminds her again. Megan waves at Mum, hoping she will go away. This time Mother feels herself getting upset. At 10:27, Mother explodes with anger. 'Hang up right now, young lady. You are restricted from the phone for two weeks.' Megan has pushed Mother's button.

Children push your buttons because they like driving you crazy. They like seeing you transformed from a rational, clear-headed, calm parent into an unreasonable, provoked maniac. One minute you are composed and sensible, the next minute you are agitated and senseless.

Every parent can relate to this. When you get angry, yell, scream or threaten, your button has been pushed. When you find yourself telling your child that he is grounded for a year, your button has been pushed.

Children push your buttons hoping you will give in and let them have their way. Children push your buttons to get attention because they want you to feel guilty and blame yourself when you punish them, because they are angry at you, or sometimes to get even and hurt you.

We all have these buttons. When they are pushed, each of us reacts in our own unique way. Usually we become angry, impulsive, and sometimes vengeful.

Two Reactions for One Misbehaviour

Twelve-year-old Sean asks his mother, Cindy, if he can have a few friends over to watch TV. Cindy says no. She explains that she has a lot of work to do tonight: 'Perhaps you can have them over some other night. Maybe next weekend.' Sean does not accept her answer. He begins to badger and whine: 'I never get to have friends over. You're not fair.' Cindy argues her point. Sean argues in return. The argument intensifies. Sean starts having a tantrum. Cindy gets angry. She yells at Sean to go to his room and stay there for the remainder of the day.

Going to his room is a punishment, so arguing should be weakened; but in reality, Sean is arguing more every day. Even though Cindy consistently sends Sean to his room every time, Sean continues to argue.

Sean argues to push Cindy's buttons. Cindy had two reactions to Sean's misbehaviour: she became angry with Sean and she punished Sean. What if making Cindy angry was part of Sean's plan? What if Cindy's anger was a payoff for Sean? Then Cindy's anger was a reward.

When Cindy punishes Sean for arguing, she concurrently rewards him for arguing. Sean trades going to his room for making Cindy upset. This gives Sean control and power. That is why Sean continues to argue each day even though Cindy punishes him consistently. *The reward of control is stronger than the punishment.* Cindy must change her behaviour. She must learn to control her anger when she punishes Sean. She must stay calm and not argue. By controlling herself, Cindy removes Sean's reward for arguing; therefore, the punishment will have more of an effect.

When some parents learn this, they respond by wanting to use stronger punishments, but large punishments combined with anger could be disastrous. Even if you use a punishment that is stronger than the reward of pushing your buttons, your anger greatly neutralizes the effects of the punishment. It will take much longer for the punishment to weaken this bad behaviour.

How to Cope with Anger, Stress and Guilt

Guilt, anger, stress, fear, anxiety, and most other unpleasant emotions, are self-defeating. Anger impairs your judgment; it rewards a power-seeking child. Guilt makes you compensate; you do not follow through. You feel sorry for not being a perfect parent, and you try to make it up to your child by giving in.

These feelings interfere with successful parenting. They inhibit your relationship with your children. They can cause misbehaviour to increase. Learning how to cope with self-defeating emotions and beliefs will increase your happiness as a person, a spouse, and a parent.

If you want to reduce the amount of negative emotions in your life, you must believe two things: you control your thoughts, and your thoughts control your emotions. Therefore, you control how you feel. You control happiness, joy and excitement. You control guilt, anger, stress and fear.

I lived for many years believing that unsafe drivers, poorly planned motorways, dead car batteries and uncapped tubes of toothpaste made me angry. I used to believe that untrained sales people and incompetent waitresses made me angry. I now realize that these circumstances are part of life. I can choose to be angry or stay calm. I prefer staying calm. I allow much less anger into my life than I did ten years ago. I still get angry. When I do, I realize what has happened and I let it go.

I once felt guilty for not having all the answers and failing to meet the needs of every parent and child that came to me for help. I now accept my humanness and imperfection. It is easy to succumb to self-defeating behaviour. Resisting it takes practice.

You will always be tempted to give in to self-defeating emotions. You will have spontaneous reactions that seem impossible to control. You might still feel guilty and angry when your child has a tantrum in public, or become discouraged if your son has a poor school report. However, you can do a lot to improve your day-to-day experience. A certain amount of child misbehaviour and aggravation is part of parenting. Children can create frustration and discouragement. Their misbehaviour can push your buttons. If your children push your buttons, take preventive action. Make a plan to protect yourself.

Defending Yourself Against Button Attacks

Some parents find it helpful to have a technique that diffuses their anger. Go and sit in your room for a few minutes. Listen to music. Make a cup of coffee. Go for a walk. Count to twenty-five. Think peaceful thoughts. Reward yourself when you do survive a button attack.

Do not expect perfection from yourself in the first week. Make your goal more realistic. If one of your children successfully pushes your buttons, do not put yourself down. Do not think that you are a failure. You are human. Do not let your disappointment keep you down. Encourage yourself just as you would encourage one of your children. Do not dwell on your inadequacies. Focus on the times that you were able to maintain your control in frustrating situations. Think about the times you were successful.

Your buttons have an important influence on the way you discipline your children. Conflicts can be resolved without anger. Stay calm. Your communication will be more effective and punishment will be more effective. If you present yourself as a model for self-control, your children will learn more effectively.

You may have to protect your buttons for weeks before you see results. Your children will test you – that's how it works. Even though you are not getting angry any more, your children will still try to push your buttons. Do not give in to their attacks.

What happens if you do give in occasionally? What happens if you still get angry once in a while? You will probably make the problem worse. You will be encouraging your children to push your buttons more, not less. That's why it is so important to protect your buttons. Be strong. Be consistent.

How to Express Anger Constructively

There will be times when you get angry. Occasional anger is normal. Do not feel guilty about it. It is okay for your children to know that you have a boiling point. It is not okay to let your anger get in the way of good discipline.

Many parents get angry but do not say or do anything about it. Instead they save it up. This is a mistake. This is the San Andreas fault syndrome. Pressure builds and builds, and then the earth quakes. We let our anger build and build until we crack. This confuses children: 'I have had two other fights with my brother today. This time Mum acts as though we killed somebody.' Do not save anger. When you save anger, it can become uncontrollable.

Let it out slowly and in small amounts. Tell your child what he did, how you feel and why you feel that way: 'When you fight like that, I get angry because you could get hurt or break something,' 'When you don't ring home, I get worried that something might have happened to you.'

Children push your buttons to get a reaction. They hope you will get upset and change your mind or give in. Do not let your emotions get the best of you. Dealing with misbehaviour as it happens helps you vent anger without blame, and thus keeps you from saving anger and then exploding. It is better for your mental health, and it is better for your children.

What Are Your Button Pushers?

Make a list of the misbehaviours that push your buttons. What misbehaviours get you angry and upset? Next, outline a plan to deal with each button pusher.

Button Pusher:

Your two children argue.

Plan:

Stay calm – do not get angry or yell.

If I get angry, go and sit in my room.

Cool off before I say anything.

Let it out slowly.

Do not save my anger until it erupts.

'I feel angry when you argue like that.'

Spotlight the positive – focus on co-operation.

Look for times when they agree.

Button Pusher: _____
_____
_____

Plan: _____
_____
_____
_____
_____

Button Pusher: _____
_____
_____

Plan: _____
_____
_____
_____
_____

Chapter 16
Use Punishments That Teach

At Brandt and Audra's house, beds need to be made before leaving for school. If you fail to make your bed, you go to bed thirty minutes early. The last time that Brandt failed to make his bed was three weeks ago. Audra fails to make her bed about four mornings a week. She is sent to bed early each time.

Most parents believe that going to bed early is a good punishment. This seems like a good plan, but look at what is actually happening. This form of punishment works well for Brandt; he avoids the punishment by remembering to make his bed. He has decided that staying up a little later is important.

Going to bed early is not a punishment for Audra. She does not avoid it. Going to bed early has had no effect on her behaviour; she is not making her bed. Maybe she likes going to bed early – I certainly do! Another punishment should be used for Audra, something that will change her behaviour.

Punishment is a negative consequence. When used properly, punishment eliminates or reduces misbehaviour. Using punishment correctly is difficult. It requires consistent follow-through. Too much punishment is harmful; it creates unpleasant feelings and drains energy. Punishment works, but it is not easy to use effectively. Most parents believe that punishing bad behaviour will stop the child from repeating the behaviour. Sometimes this is true, but sometimes it is not:

'How do you punish your children?'
'I yell.'
'How do your children react to your yelling?'
'They don't react. They usually ignore me.'
'Then what?'
'I get angry. Sometimes I yell again.'
'Do they stop?'
'For a while, maybe.'
'What do you try next?'
'Sometimes I spank them.'
'How often do you have to spank them?'
'About eight or ten times a day.'

Any punishment that is used this often is not working. The behaviour is not getting better. The children are not listening to the yelling. They are not avoiding the spankings.

Good Punishments Are Seldom Used

A true punishment is one that is seldom used because it is seldom needed. This is punishment's golden rule. Punishment should reduce the need for more punishment; it should decrease the misbehaviour. If the misbehaviour does not change, then the punishment is not working. Many parents make this mistake, focusing on the punishment rather than the misbehaviour. If you punish your child five or six times a day for the same misbehaviour, the punishment is not working. If you keep adding to the punishment and the misbehaviour continues, punishment is not working. It is not the punishment that is important but the misbehaviour. A punishment must change the misbehaviour. If it doesn't, try something else. You may think that yelling, threatening, scolding and spanking are good punishments. These reactions release your anger, but they are not good punishments; they have little long-term effect on misbehaviour. Anger and punishment do not mix.

Do Not Punish When You Are Angry

Linda hurried home one day to take her dog to the vet. When she arrived home, she heard someone in the house. She was ready to run next door and call the police when she heard a giggle. She called out. There was another giggle. She went into her thirteen-year-old daughter's bedroom. Another giggle. Nancie and two friends were hiding in the closet, skipping school. Linda was so angry she could not think straight. All she could say was, 'Nancie, it's going to take me and your father a few days to think about how you will be punished for this.' Linda did not let her anger get in the way of being rational and making a good judgment. Allowing her daughter to worry for a few days is a pretty good punishment all by itself.

Whenever I do a workshop on punishment, I explain this next point carefully. For many parents, this is an idea with considerable impact. When you punish in anger, you are actually doing two things at the same time – punishing and reacting with anger. What if your child intended to get you angry? What if your child wanted to get even or retaliate because of something that happened earlier? Seeing you get angry is not a punishment. It is a reward! When you get angry at misbehaviour, you are teaching your child how to have control over your emotional state of mind. You are giving your child power over you. This is a payoff; the misbehaviour is reinforced, not punished. As a result, the misbehaviour increases. The effects of the punishment are negated by the reward of getting you angry. Some children would trade a smack on the bottom for the power they receive when they have succeeded in getting you angry. The only way to break this cycle of retaliation is to stop punishing with anger. If you find yourself getting angry, walk away. Dispense with your anger first, then confront the misbehaviour. Do not let your children push your buttons.

Do not punish when you are angry. Cool off first. The purpose of punishment is to teach your children to behave better in the future, not to get even. Sometimes your children can make you very angry, but this is not the time to hand out punishment. I remember a child who was upset because he was grounded forever. When I spoke with his dad, he explained that the boy had lost some of his tools. He got so angry at his son, he grounded him for the rest of his life. He over-reacted.

When you over-react because you are angry, you may say things that you do not mean. You cannot ground a child for life. Do not punish when you are angry. You will be teaching your children that punishment is a form of revenge.

The purpose of punishment is to change misbehaviour and teach better decision making. Punishment is most effective when it is predetermined and planned. Punishment does not work well as an impulsive reaction. When you become angry, you are acting as a model for negative behaviour. You will not be teaching your children to make better decisions.

Do Not Punish to Embarrass

Punishment should not embarrass, humiliate or degrade children. Punishment is meant to teach your child that misbehaving is not a good decision and behaving is a good decision. When punishment embarrasses your child, it creates unhealthy feelings. The embarrassment will only cause your child to think of you as mean or unfair. When this occurs, your child will not learn to make better decisions. He will not learn co-operation. Your child may strike back in anger, which can start a negative cycle.

Do not punish your child in front of other children. Take your child aside. Tell him what he has done and that he will be punished. Talk about it later, when the two of you are alone.

Use Punishment Consistently

Punishment must be administered consistently. Once you decide to punish a misbehaviour, do so always. If you punish only when you feel like it, you will make the problem worse. Once you tell your child that he is going to be punished, follow through. You must use punishment consistently, even after you have had a long, miserable day. You can never miss or let the misbehaviour slide – not even once. Many parents make this mistake. Children love it. It motivates them to test you – to see if you will punish them this time.

Angela wanted to know why punishment did not have any effect on her son, Bryan. She explained that she 'tried everything. Nothing bothers him. He never does what I ask him to do.' After more discussion, I learned that Angela punishes Brian once or twice a week, while he did what he pleased all the other times. Angela did not follow through consistently; Bryan could misbehave several times a day and only be punished once or twice a week. This is a trade-off most children would make gladly. Angela and Bryan were trapped in a pattern. She did not punish consistently because she believed it did not work. He continued to misbehave because he got away with it most of the time. Angela worked out a plan that used positive feedback and punishment, and emphasized co-operation and good decisions. She used small punishments, but she used them consistently. As Angela's behaviour improved, Bryan's behaviour improved.

Be Reasonable

Punishment must be reasonable. Short and simple punishments are more effective than harsh punishments. React appropriately to the size of the misbehaviour. Do not restrict your son for a month because he did not finish his vegetables. Take away his dessert. When punishments are reasonable, children learn what kinds of behaviour are important.

Punishment should be administered as soon after the misbehaviour as possible. The more immediate, the more effective the punishment will be. This is especially true with young children. The only exception to this rule occurs when you are angry. Do not punish immediately when you are angry. Wait until you calm down, just as Linda did when she caught Nancie skipping school. You might say, 'You will be punished for this, but I have to cool down first.'

With misbehaviour that is recurrent, punishment should only be used after you have tried several positive remedies. Most adults think of punishment first. Most adults think that you always treat misbehaviour with a punishment. You can improve misbehaviour by using positive feedback to strengthen the opposite of the misbehaviour. Your two children argue constantly. Instead of saying, 'If you do not stop fighting, you will both be grounded for the weekend,' point out the opposite. The opposite of arguing is co-operating. Use encouragement and positive feedback when they are co-operating and sharing: 'It's good to see you having fun. You should be proud of yourselves for the way you are sharing the computer.' Immediately resorting to punishment traps many parents. No one likes how it feels. One way to escape this trap is to focus on positive behaviour.

Your Turn

Pam cannot understand why Steven will not behave. Pam wants to be more positive but sometimes forgets. Steven is a very active child. He gets into things he is not supposed to touch. Whenever Steven does not mind, Pam becomes upset and frustrated. Pam yells a lot. She spanks too. Nothing seems to work. What can you tell Pam about her behaviour?

Pam needs to realize that her style of punishment is not working. Steven has become immune to the yelling and the spanking, and his misbehaviour is not improving. Pam needs to control herself. Getting angry and frustrated is only aggravating the situation. Her anger may be rewarding to Steven. Most of all, Pam must remember to be positive. The strongest tool she has is positive feedback.

Punishment works, but it is not easy to use. Positive feedback is much easier to use and more fun to use. Positive feedback creates internal motivation in children. It teaches self-discipline and promotes a healthy and pleasant family climate. Successful parents emphasize the positive. Positive feedback, extinction and punishment are always in effect, whether you are conscious of them or not. The key to successful parenting is to be aware of these principles and use them to your advantage.

Parents who are only interested in controlling misbehaviour will punish. Parents who want children to be co-operative will balance positive feedback with extinction and redirection and use a minimal amount of punishment. If you emphasize the positive, you will only need a minimal amount of punishment.

The next four pages are refrigerator pages – make photocopies and hang them on the refrigerator. The first page is a list of questions to ask yourself about the way you use punishment. The second page is a summary of strategies that strengthen or weaken behaviour. The next two pages are a comparison between positive feedback and punishment. Many parents have told me that an occasional review of these pages helps them keep a positive focus. I hope they do the same for you.

Ten Questions to Ask When You Use Punishment

1. Will this punishment teach my child better decision-making skills?
2. Does this punishment change the misbehaviour?
3. Does this punishment reduce the need for more punishment?
4. Am I getting angry when I punish?
5. Is this punishment part of a plan? Do I use it impulsively?

6. Am I getting even? Will this punishment humiliate or embarrass my child?
7. Am I being consistent?
8. Will I follow through immediately (except when I am angry)?
9. Is this punishment reasonable and fair?
10. Have I tried positive remedies first?

How to Strengthen or Weaken Behaviour

To strengthen good behaviour:

Use positive feedback.

Examples:
When your children behave, reward them by thanking them. When you see your children sharing, tell them that they should be proud of themselves.

To reduce misbehaviour:

1. Use positive feedback to strengthen the opposite behaviour.

Examples:
If you want to reduce the amount of arguing between two children, call attention to the time when they are not arguing.
If your children have a negative attitude, reward anything positive.

2. Use extinction to eliminate any rewards for misbehaviour.

Examples:
Do not give in to your children's demands.
Ignore your children when they try to get your attention in a negative way.

3. Use punishment.

Examples:

>A child who comes home late cannot go out the next day.
>
>A child who does not do his chores forfeits part of his pocket money.

A Comparison Between Positive Feedback and Punishment

Positive feedback feels good to give and receive.	Punishment creates unpleasant feelings, often anger.
Positive feedback emphasizes good behaviour. It teaches children to think.	Punishment draws attention to misbehaviour.
Positive feedback increases motivation.	Punishment can have a negative effect on - motivation.
Positive feedback creates feelings of success.	Punishment can cause children to feel like failures.
Positive feedback improves a child's self-esteem.	Punishment can have a negative impact on self-esteem.
Positive feedback gives children self-confidence.	Punishment weakens self-confidence.
Positive feedback teaches children to trust their decisions.	Punishment does not teach trust. It sometimes teaches fear.

Positive feedback motivates children to seek goals.	Punishment may cause children to feel despair: 'Why try? I always get into trouble anyway.'
Positive feedback develops responsibility: 'When I make good decisions, I feel good.'	Punishment often teaches children to avoid admitting responsibility for their actions.
Positive feedback promotes healthy family relationships.	Punishment may alienate family members.
Positive feedback encourages children to talk to their parents.	Punishment discourages children from talking to their parents.
Positive feedback teaches children to be positive with others.	Punishment that is aggressive teaches children to be aggressive towards others.
Positive feedback is easy to use effectively.	Punishment is difficult to use easily.

Chapter 17
How To Punish Your Children Without Punishing Yourself

It was late in the afternoon on July 4. We had planned to go to the evening fireworks display. Our children were arguing more than usual. I threatened them, hoping they would stop: 'If you don't quit arguing, we are not going to the fireworks.' What a foolish thing to say. If they did not go, we did not go; there was no way we would have found a baby-sitter at 5:00 pm on the Fourth of July, as every teenager in town was going to the fireworks. The children did not stop, and we did not go. We were punished along with our children.

A better punishment would have been to separate them when they started arguing, and make them play alone. I did not think. I got angry and made a foolish threat that ended up costing me more than my children. Think carefully before talking. Anger can get you in trouble. Think about how the punishment will affect you and the rest of the family. Will this punishment disrupt me? If you have a child who likes to control you or others in the family, choose his punishments carefully. Be sure that the punishment only affects the child who misbehaved and not anyone else. Do not say, 'We are not going until you clean your room.' If you are going somewhere he wants to go, this threat may work. If he does not want to go, you have just given your child a lot of power. No one can go until the room is clean. You are giving this child control over the entire family. Who is being punished?

What do you do with your child who is not permitted to go somewhere with the rest of the family? Get a baby-sitter and then go and have a good time. You may want your child to pay for some or all of the cost of the baby-sitter. Your child will learn that his misbehaviour will not prevent the family from having fun. Select punishments that impact your child, not you. Your other children will learn something too. Misbehaviour only affects the one who misbehaves.

Parents often wonder how to take TV privileges from one child. If they have to switch off the TV, the other children will be punished. That's true. Do not switch the TV off because one child is restricted. That punishes everyone. Watch TV as usual. The child who is being punished has to go in another room. That's the true punishment. If no one can watch TV because he cannot watch TV, you are giving your child control over the entire family. Who is being punished?

Use Punishments That Are Easy to Enforce

Choose punishments that you can enforce easily. This will enable you to follow through. If a punishment is inconvenient or laborious, you will be less consistent. A father told me that he would lock up the video game for three hours whenever his son would disobey:

> 'How often do you lock up the game?'
> 'Once or twice a week.'
> 'Does your son obey on all the other days?'

'If he did, would I be talking with you?'

'Why don't you lock up the game every time he
    disobeys?'

'If I locked that game up every time he did not do
    what he was supposed to do, I would be locking
    that thing up ten times a day.'

'Why don't you do that?'

'It would take me forever with all those cables
    and plugs.'

Dad is using a punishment that is inconvenient, so he does
not follow through consistently. His son is not learning to
obey; he is learning that he can disobey as often as he likes and
only lose his game once or twice a week. Dad has probably
identified an effective punishment – taking away the video
game – but he needs to be more consistent. He needs to lock up
the game every time. If the video game cables make this punishment cumbersome, then Dad needs a more effective way of
administering the punishment.

Explain the Punishment

Tell your child the purpose of the punishment. When you explain punishment, you increase your child's understanding and
co-operation. Explain that you are on his side. You are not the
enemy. You are trying to help him make better decisions in the
future:

'I am not trying to hurt you or make you angry. You
are being punished because you made a poor choice
about your behaviour. I want you to learn from this
so you will think differently next time. I do not want
you to think I am out to get you. I am not. I am out
to help you.'

Explain that you are not trying to get even. Ignore irritating
comments such as, 'You expect me to believe you are doing this

for me. Sure you are.' Only explain it once. Do not become caught in lengthy explanations and arguments.

Use Punishments That Are Realistic

Select punishments that fit the crime. Use reality consequences. A child who makes a mess cleans the mess. A child who pees in the refrigerator should clean the refrigerator. A child who carelessly breaks something should fix it or work to pay for it. A child who comes home late should not go out the next day. A child who does not put his dirty clothes in the laundry basket does his own washing. Children who can operate CD players, videos, and computers can operate a washing machine. These examples illustrate consequences that are relevant to the misbehaviour. They have more meaning to your child. They help teach a lesson.

Some children can be trusted to choose their punishment. This helps them learn more quickly. It shows them that you want to be fair, and it encourages them to be mature and responsible:

> 'Your behaviour has been very good until this incident. I am going to trust you to choose your own punishment for this misbehaviour. I know you will be fair and just. Let me know what you decide.'

Bigger Does Not Mean Better

Mild punishments are usually more productive than harsh punishments. Keep things in perspective. Don't bring out a cannon to get your children to hang up the towels. Punishments that are short and sweet teach better lessons. Large punishments often create feelings of anger or revenge. When your child feels angry, little learning takes place. When your child believes that you have been unjust in your use of punishment, your child often retaliates or argues. This can start a negative cycle. You punish, your child becomes angry and retaliates by misbehaving again, maybe worse than before. You punish again, perhaps a little more severely, just to make your point. Your child becomes more angry and retaliates by misbehaving again. I have worked with families where the parents were punishing their children for things that happened months ago:

'How long have you been grounded?'

'Since the beginning of last term.'

'How long is that?'

'About five months.'

'What are you grounded from?'

'Everything. No dates. No friends. No TV. No phone calls. No stereo. No anything. My parents want me to sit in my room every night and study.'

'Is that what you do?'

'I sneak out my window after they go to bed.'

'What did you do to get your parents so upset they would ground you for five months?'

'They didn't ground me for five months at first.'

'What do you mean?'

'It started with no phone calls for a month.'

'What happened?'

'I didn't think it was fair. So I used the phone when they weren't around.'

'And – ?'

'And I got caught.'

'So then your parents made it longer.'

'They made it two months and added that no friends could come over.'

'Did you think that was fair?'

'Just for using the phone! That wasn't fair in the first place.'

'I think I know the rest.'

'It just kept getting worse and worse.'

'Was it worth being grounded most of your second year?'

'Well – no. But I'm not giving up now.'

Using Restriction Constructively

Restriction is a useful punishment for children and adolescents. Being grounded is a type of restriction. Restriction means loss of one or more privileges for a specific length of time. You will have to determine what the privilege should be. Some examples are loss of TV time, going to bed early, being restricted from seeing friends, no telephone, no video games, no toys, and so on. Choose a restriction that is easy to enforce and that impacts the offender and no one else.

Restricting children for misbehaviour is a popular form of punishment. Unfortunately, few parents use restriction effectively. Most parents begin with a period of time that is too long. As adults, we forget that a week or two can be forever to a child. Long periods of restriction are often the result of an argument, hurt feelings, or anger, and they can backfire, causing your child to feel persecuted or picked on. This can turn into feelings of revenge, and a cycle of retaliation begins.

There is a built-in problem with restriction. Many children who become grounded or restricted feel there is no hope. Without hope, there is little reason to behave: 'Why behave? I can't go out for a week anyway.' Then the child decides that everyone else should be just as miserable.

There is a workable solution to this problem. If you decide to restrict your child, choose an even number of days. Choose four, six, eight or twelve days, depending on the seriousness of the offence and the age of your child. Twelve days is usually the maximum effective period – anything longer and you run the risk of retaliation. Next, explain that each good day will result in one day taken off the end of the restriction period. Let's assume that you have restricted your child for six days, Wednesday through to Monday. If your child has a good day on Wednesday, then drop Monday. If Thursday is a good day, then drop Sunday. If things go well on Friday, then drop Saturday. Friday is the last day of restriction. You may want to draw a chart or calendar so that your child can cross off days and see his progress.

This technique works extremely well. It lets your child know that you want to be fair, even though you mean business. It also lets your child know that you expect proper behaviour even while he is restricted. Being restricted is not a licence to be unco-operative. Most of all, this approach gives your child a strong incentive to behave immediately – no sitting around the house being miserable for a week.

The success of this strategy depends on how well you define a good day. Then stick to what you say. It helps a great deal to write down what you require.

Rules for dropping a day:

> Do what you are asked.
>
> Speak in a pleasant voice.
>
> Be kind and polite to your sister.

Be sure that a good day is truly a good day. Do not drop a day unless it is deserved. If you drop days too easily, you will be defeating the purpose of this approach. Your child can be restricted and still earn other activities. For example, your child could be restricted from the telephone and still be earning a contract for a new CD. I have worked with preschool teachers who have modified this technique. They use minute restrictions. When a child misuses a toy, the child is restricted from the toy for ten minutes. If the child behaves, he can earn the toy back in five minutes.

Chapter 18
Spanking

'My kids don't listen to anything I say.'
'What do you do?'
'I spank them. Even though I know it's wrong. I'm
    always mad at them and then I get mad at myself.
    I can't live this way. There must be something else
    I can do.'

About 10 per cent of parents spank their children and see nothing wrong with spanking. About 20 per cent of parents never spank their children. About 70 per cent of parents spank their children but wish they didn't. The last sentence says a lot. Many parents want a better way of punishing their children. Parents want to manage their children's misbehaviour without getting angry and without spanking.

Does spanking work? Are there any damaging effects? These questions have no exact answers. Even professionals disagree about the value of spanking. Some people argue that spanking works. Others argue that it does not. No wonder many parents are confused about spanking. Spanking is a form of punishment – but is it an acceptable way to punish children?

That is for you to decide. This chapter enables you to evaluate the practice of spanking. The first part of this chapter will explain the risks and pitfalls associated with spanking, while the remainder presents three ways that parents use spanking, along with some precautions.

What Happens When You Spank

A spanking usually stops a child's misbehaviour. When the misbehaviour stops, the parent feels rewarded and learns that spanking works. A spanking can result in good behaviour just as a chocolate bar can buy peace and quiet in the supermarket. Using chocolate to stop a tantrum is a temporary solution – you will be feeding your child a lot of chocolate to keep him quiet in the future. In the same way, spanking is a temporary solution.

A child who is spanked will usually settle down and behave. After a while, the child acts up again. The parent spanks again because the spanking seemed to work the first time. The child is good for a while and then misbehaves again. The parent spanks again, and so on. This pattern snares many parents.

This pattern occurs because spanking provides external control of children. It does not encourage children to make responsible decisions or promote internal decision making. It teaches children to behave 'or else'. Children who are frequently spanked do not learn self-control. An eight-year-old once told me that he could misbehave as long as he wanted: 'My Mum spanks me when I have to stop.'

Spanking is not a good punishment because it happens in a second or two and it's over. Most children would rather have a smack than lose a special privilege for a few days. The spanking is over quickly, and they can be off on new adventures. Many children believe that once they have been spanked everything is okay: 'We are even.' Spanking causes many children to focus on the punishment rather than on their poor decision.

Problems can arise in families where one parent spanks and the other doesn't. This can cause children to avoid the parent who spanks. This avoidance interferes with normal parent-child development. Children see the parent who does not spank as being unable to manage. The children will continue to misbehave for this parent. Children avoid the parent who spanks, and see the parent who does not spank as weak. This means that both parents lose.

Spankings have side effects. Spankings are embarrassing, and embarrassment causes children to get angry or think about retaliation. It seldom teaches children to think about how they could have made a better decision. Spankings can affect a child's attitude; children who are frequently spanked feel insecure. They do not trust themselves: 'If I do the wrong thing, I will be hit.' Many children who are spanked have poor self-esteem. Some children withdraw. Others become excitable, overactive, and aggressive.

Three Ways Parents Use Spanking

The Impulsive Approach

There are three ways that parents use spanking to punish their children: the impulsive approach, the angry approach and the planned approach. The impulsive approach is also known as the 'all day long' method. A mother once said, 'I spank him and spank him and spank him and he still will not listen.' He is not listening because the spankings have become meaningless.

The impulsive approach is more commonly used with younger children. These parents are never too serious about the actual smack. They usually grab the child with one hand and swing with the other. The smack is almost automatic or reflexive. The child hollers and then carries on playing. This is also known as the 'Barbershop syndrome'. You have seen parents spank their children five times or more in the thirty minutes they needed to wait their turn for a haircut.

Many parents use a technique called slap-the-toddler-on-the-hand. Young children like to experiment. They like to touch things to see what happens. When they touch something they shouldn't, they get slapped. Slaps do not teach. Explain why an object should not be touched and remove the child or the object. Your children copy you. When you slap, they learn to slap.

The impulsive approach has no lasting effect on a child's misbehaviour. After being spanked on the bottom a few dozen times, the smack becomes meaningless. For these parents, spanking is a continuous reaction. These parents do not know any alternative. They think that spanking is what you are obliged to do when your children misbehave: 'That's the only way I can get her to behave.' They believe they are doing the proper thing to be good parents.

Do children learn anything from the impulsive approach? Nothing that will teach them to make better decisions. Far too often, the spanking depends on how the parent feels at that given moment. If you are short-tempered today, your children get spanked for every little thing they do. If you are feeling more tolerant, your children get away with murder. This inconsistency confuses children: 'I did this yesterday and it was okay. Today, I'm getting a spanking.' It teaches children to be sneaky. It does not teach them right from wrong or how to make better decisions.

Children who are impulsively and frequently spanked believe that hitting is a normal part of life. So when another child does something they do not like, they hit. This becomes a problem with siblings, at school and with playmates. When children hit each other, they get into trouble. This confuses children. When adults hit, it's okay. But when children hit, it's not okay.

Children who are frequently spanked believe that everything they do is wrong. This creates poor self-esteem and a lack of self-confidence. The goal of good discipline is to teach our children to make responsible decisions. Frequent spankings do not promote this; they teach children to have poor self-control and to behave because of fear. If you do not behave, you are spanked. When the parent is not around to provide external control, the child has no control at all.

The impulsive approach is not an effective punishment because it does not minimize the need for future spankings but in fact perpetuates this need. Frequent spankings model negative behaviour. They are reactive. They are never planned. Parents who use the impulsive approach seldom use positive remedies to change misbehaviour.

The Angry Approach

The second way that parents use spanking is the angry approach. This approach is the most common as well as the most harmful. When you become angry and spank your child, a number of problems result. You teach your child how to push your buttons. This teaches your child that his misbehaviour has power over your self-control. Spanking in anger is impulsive. It is always a reaction. When you spank in anger, you could become carried away and may hurt your child.

When you spank in anger, you create intense negative emotions. You create these emotions in yourself, your child and the rest of the family. These emotions can damage your child's self-esteem. Many children begin to fear their parents. They begin to mistrust their parents, which leads to a lack of self-trust.

Spanking in anger teaches children to strike out when they are angry. It teaches children that when they are angry, they do not have to exercise self-control, because you do not show self-control when you are angry. Spanking in anger does not teach children how to make better decisions.

When you spank in anger, you are often vengeful. You let your frustration build until it explodes. Then, you retaliate with revenge, sometimes humiliating and embarrassing your child. Children learn they are a source of frustration to you.

If your anger has you trapped in a pattern of spanking, make a commitment to stop. This will take plenty of self-control and rethinking, but it is a habit worth changing.

The Planned Approach

The third way that some parents use spanking is the planned approach. This approach means that you tell your child that certain kinds of behaviour will result in a smack. For example, 'If you use bad language, you will be punished by getting a smack.' If your child uses bad language, calmly administer a smack. The key word in the last sentence is 'calmly'. If you do not stay calm, then you are using the angry approach. The planned approach is also known as, 'This hurts me more than it does you'.

When you use spanking as part of a total plan, it is more effective than when you use it impulsively. However, consider these factors before you use the planned approach. There is no evidence to show that planned spankings teach children to be more responsible. Planned spankings still model negative behaviour. If you allow yourself to spank, you may get angry when you spank. You may use spanking inconsistently because of your mood or because you feel guilty, and inconsistency makes the problem worse. Many parents forget that a plan should include positive solutions. They plan to use a spanking as a punishment, but do not plan positive strategies. They forget that the plan should emphasize the positive and not the negative.

I have never known a professional who approved of the impulsive or angry approach. Some professionals approve of the planned approach; but if you are going to take the time and energy to implement a plan, why not develop a plan that is positive? Develop a plan that uses other forms of punishment, such as restriction or time-out (see page 147).

You can raise self-disciplined children without spanking. Spanking may be a good release for your anger or frustration, but it is a temporary solution that does not teach responsibility and can do more harm than good. If you choose to use spanking, use the planned approach. Use a plan that emphasizes the positive; a plan that enables you to maintain your self-control; a plan that gets results.

Chapter 19
Correcting Misbehaviour with Time-Out

Judy was twenty-two but looked much older. She had four children, the oldest six years old. She was five months pregnant and had no time for herself. There was fatigue in her voice. Her four-year-old son, Randy, was driving her crazy. She was not able to manage his tantrums and demands. With tears of desperation, she told how she spent most of her time: 'All I do is yell. He never does anything I ask. He just runs around the house making a mess. I don't have time for my other children because of him. I have to do something before this baby is born.' After learning about time-out, Judy knew she had a tool – one that would work.

Time-out is an effective method. It is a replacement for yelling, scolding, threatening and spanking. A time-out prevents your children from pushing your buttons. To use a time-out means to place your child in a dull and boring place for a few minutes. It means time away from the group, time away from the fun. A time-out means that your child spends time away from anything positive. Being denied activity is a kind of punishment.

Judy went home and prepared. Randy began the next morning as usual. He refused to come to the breakfast table. Judy put him in time-out. Judy told him to sit quietly for five minutes; then he could come out. Randy refused to be quiet. He screamed, yelled, cried and did everything that an enraged four-year-old child can imagine. He was in time-out for an hour and a half. Judy did not give up. She stayed calm and she was consistent. Finally, he sat quietly for five minutes. He came out and had his breakfast. It was ten o'clock.

Judy's second battle occurred just after noon. Randy refused to lower the volume on the television when asked. Judy placed him in time-out. His resistance was weaker, his will was not as strong, and his tantrum less violent. He was in time-out for only twenty minutes.

Judy used time-outs on several other occasions that first week. It became easier to use each time. She trusted time-outs. In return, it gave her confidence. Her son was less defiant. Within two weeks, her son was listening. Judy was managing him without screaming and chasing.

Three-year-old Laura was a bedtime procrastinator. Laura began screaming and having a tantrum as soon as Donna mentioned bedtime. Pyjamas were wrestled on every night. Nagging followed the pyjamas: 'Can I have a drink of water?' 'Would you read me a story?' 'There is something wrong with my pillow.' Donna believed that these bedtime battles were not caused by any fears, but because Laura wanted to have power and control.

Donna used time-out to get Laura to bed. If Laura argued or began whining, she would go to time-out. If Laura refused to go to bed in any way, she would go to time-out. Donna was consistent. When Laura argued or whined, Donna put her in time-out. Then every five minutes, Donna would ask Laura if she was ready to go to bed. After fifteen or twenty minutes of sitting alone, Laura was ready to go to bed. In two weeks, Donna sent me a note: 'I am beginning to think of the way I disciplined Laura in two ways, before time-out and after time-out. The difference is fantastic. Bedtime is so easy now. She never gets upset or argues. Even when my older children stay up later than she does.'

Why does time-out work so well? It works because it gives you a tool to back up what you say. Time-out is a teaching technique, a mild punishment that you administer quickly and easily. Time-out works because children do not like it, and will behave to avoid it. Here is an overview.

The first step is to select the right setting. Next, choose one misbehaviour that you want to eliminate. Finally, explain time-out to your child. Describe the behaviour that must stop. Explain that this behaviour will result in a time-out. You will need a timer that sounds a bell or a buzzer. An oven timer works well, as long as your child can hear it from where they are spending their time-out. It may help to have two timers. One for the child to see and one for you. Explain that yours is the official clock! Each of these steps is explained later in this chapter.

There are other aspects of this method that you need to understand for time-outs to be most effective. Time-out is most useful for children between the ages of two and twelve. With caution, you can use time-out with children who are younger than two years old. You can use time-out with children as old as fourteen, but it may not be as effective. Reality consequences (see chapter 8) and restriction (see chapter 17) are more appropriate punishments for teenagers.

Use time-out with determination and planning, not impulsively. Your child must be able to predict when they might receive time-out. Your child must understand when and how you will use time-out. If you use it for arguing, do not send your child to time-out for messing up the family room. Choose a more suitable punishment, such as cleaning the family room or other rooms in the house. Your child needs to understand how time-out will work in advance of its initial use. Never use time-out as a surprise.

Use time-out consistently. Once you have said that time-out will punish a misbehaviour, do so always – no exceptions. Do not slack off, give in or make excuses. If you do not follow through, even once, you will make the problem worse. You will be creating more work for yourself in the future.

Remain cool and calm when you use time-out. If you let your child push your buttons, time-out will not work. If you get angry, time-out will not work. If you find yourself yelling and screaming when you use time-out, it will not work. If your child succeeds in getting you upset, the effects of time-out will be weakened. If you feel a surge of anger, walk away. Calm down. Then return to the situation. I knew a father who put himself in time-out until he cooled off. He would go for a walk or lie down for a while. He knew that interacting with his children when he was angry always had bad results.

The initial episodes of time-out may be difficult. Some children spend over an hour in time-out on the first few occasions. Early in my career I worked at a home for boys. A child spent two hours in time-out one day. He had misbehaved and needed to sit quietly for ten minutes. He chose to yell and scream obscenities for two hours before he sat quietly for ten minutes. We hated to hear this child in such a rage, but he had to learn that his tantrums would not work. He had to learn to follow the rules.

Some children really work you over in the beginning. Be prepared, particularly if your child has been getting his way for the last four or eight or ten years. Please be assured that after the first few episodes, time-out gets easier for everyone. There will be a day when your child no longer becomes angry when sent to time-out. There will be a day when you will not need time-out at all.

Using time-outs must be part of a total plan to improve your children's behaviour, but they should be only a small part of the plan. The larger part of the plan should emphasize the positive aspects of your children's behaviour. Focus 90 per cent of your energy on positive behaviour. Catch your children being good. If you take the positive for granted, improvements in your child's behaviour will not occur. If you use time-outs to correct misbehaviour and forget to reinforce good behaviour, time-outs will not be effective. Without the positive emphasis, using time-out by itself will not work. It will not make a lasting change. Time-out will become another form of punishment that your child will learn to tolerate.

Choosing the Best Setting for Time-Out

The setting for time-out needs to be boring. Most bedrooms are like recreation centres. Use a bathroom, laundry room, utility room or spare bedroom. Use a room with light. Whichever room you select, make it dull. You may want to put a chair in the room. Remove all opportunities for self-amusement. Remove all dangerous items and breakable objects. Remove anything that is valuable. For most children, you will only need to follow these precautions for three weeks or less. Once your children have learned the procedures for time-outs, you may gradually become more trusting.

Many parents have concerns about placing their child in a separate room with the door closed. This is usually more of a problem for the parent than the child. If you do not feel comfortable with the door being closed, you may try leaving it ajar. The risk here is that your child can get up and peep out, make noises for you to hear, listen to other children having fun, and so on. If your child is willing to comply with time-outs with the door ajar, there is no problem. Explain to your child that the door can be left ajar as long as he remains quiet and co-operative. If he begins to act up, the door will be closed. Some parents have used a gate across the bathroom doorway. This is permissible as long as your child does his time-out without manipulating.

Time-out is worth the planning and preparing. The setting for time-outs must be completely safe. Make your time-out room as childproof as possible. Remove anything that might cause harm. Your child must believe that you are confident about the room being safe. Eliminate any doubts that make you feel uncomfortable. Your child may use these doubts against you, saying, 'I'm scared. I'm afraid to be alone in here.' Do not let these statements influence you into letting your child out before the time is up. Tell your child, 'There is nothing in the bathroom that will hurt you.' It may be helpful to sit in the time-out room yourself for several minutes. Look around. Pretend you are an angry child. Think of what could you say or do to make Mum or Dad never want to put you in time-out again?

You may have to withstand pressure from friends and relatives. Adults who are unfamiliar with time-outs may regard them as cruel. It's ironic that many parents who see time-outs as mean see nothing wrong with spanking. Do not be influenced by this. I have never known of a child who suffered emotional damage from sitting alone for ten minutes.

Many parents use the bathroom for time-outs. A spare bathroom is preferable. Bathrooms are sturdy and contain few amusements. If you use the bathroom, remember, safety first. Remove all the medicines and all dangerous items such as razors and electrical appliances, and don't forget to remove the toilet paper.

Steven used the bathroom for time-outs with five-year-old Lynn. When he thought he had done everything to make the bathroom safe and boring, Lynn entertained herself by playing with the water in the toilet bowl. A little creativity goes a long way: Steven's remedy was to put a clamp on the toilet lid. He did not abandon the whole idea of time-outs just because there was a setback. He did not say what many parents might have said: 'She is just having fun. Time-outs don't work.' He worked through the problem. He was committed to making them work.

There is one caution about the bathroom. Do not use the bathroom as your time-out setting for a child who is being toilet trained; this would be confusing. Do not use the bathroom for time-outs with any child when another child is being toilet trained. You do not want your toddler to perceive the bathroom as a bad place. Use a utility room or spare bedroom, or your bedroom as a last resort.

Do not use a chair in the corner or a chair in the hall. Your child will learn that squirming, making faces, rocking, singing, humming, and kicking the chair legs are all excellent ways of getting you angry. Time-out needs to take place away from everyone else. A separate room is best. Kim used the couch for time-out. When her daughter would not sit, Kim would sit next to her and hold her down. This arrangement gave her daughter plenty of power. Her daughter was in charge of time-out, not Kim.

The Time in Time-Out

How long your child spends in a time-out depends on three factors. The first factor is your child's age. For children between the ages of two and three, one or two minutes in time-out is enough. For children between the ages of three and five, two or three minutes in time-out is enough. For children five and older, use five minutes.

Be consistent about the time, even though young children do not always understand the concept of time. Use a timer. An egg timer works well. The child can see the sand falling. This helps keep them occupied. Long time-outs are no better than brief time-outs. The length of time-outs does not change misbehaviour; using time-out consistently does.

The second factor is the seriousness of the misbehaviour. Manage most misbehaviours equally. Such problem behaviours as arguing, disobedience, improper language or poor manners would all be five-minute time-outs. If you feel that fighting is more serious, perhaps ten minutes would be the rule. Keep it simple. Use five minutes for most misbehaviours. Use eight or ten minutes for one or two serious misbehaviours.

The third factor is how well your child co-operates. Being unco-operative adds more time. You want time-outs to work as smoothly as possible. If the standard time-out is five minutes, the time is five minutes only if your child goes to time-out willingly and sits quietly. If your child struggles on the way to time-out, double the time. Double the time only once. How to handle a child who refuses to go to time-out is discussed in the next chapter.

If your child screams or has a tantrum while in time-out, ignore it. Do not start the timer until he is quiet. Simply tell your child that he has five (or ten) minutes and that you will start the timer when he is quiet. I tell children to knock on the door when they are ready to start their time. All the time spent yelling and having a tantrum does not count. This is how some children end up spending an hour or more in time-outs.

Children cry when they are unhappy. If your child whimpers a little, ignore it and let the timer continue to run. Ignore any singing, humming, storytelling or poetry recitals. Do not start the timer if your child can be heard throughout the house. Treat this as an outburst. The rule is: if your child is sobbing, singing or making noises to amuse himself, let the timer run. But if he is trying to get you upset, do not start the timer. Wait for him to become quiet. Tell him to notify you when he is ready to start the time.

The Priority Misbehaviour

A priority misbehaviour is a specific action that you consider inappropriate or problematic. It is a priority because you want to deal with it now. It is a misbehaviour that you want your child to stop doing. The priority misbehaviour you select must be very specific. Examples of specific misbehaviours are fighting, arguing, talking back and swearing. Terms such as obnoxious, mean and rude are not good priority misbehaviours. These terms are not specific; they do not describe the misbehaviour in a meaningful way. We all understand what these terms mean in a general sense. The problem is, these terms can be misinterpreted and create arguments. What is obnoxious to you may not be obnoxious to your child.

You may need to practise being specific. If your children misbehave a lot, it is easy to lose sight of the actual misbehaviour: 'My child is always in trouble,' 'He never does anything the way I want him to,' 'She never has a good day,' 'He gets so obnoxious I could scream,' 'That child will never behave.' If you find yourself thinking this way, consider exactly what it is that your child does. Carmen will not do things when asked. Francis hits his sister. Clint does not do his chores on time.

When the priority misbehaviour occurs, tell your child

what he has done and send him to time-out. Stay calm. Be firm and assertive.

> MUM: Greg, would you please take out the rubbish?
>
> GREG: I don't feel like it. I'll do it later.
>
> MUM: Greg, that is not obeying. Go to time-out. You have five minutes.

Once you tell your child that he has earned a time-out, do not change your mind. Some children will suddenly become obedient and co-operative, hoping you will be lenient. Do not be fooled.

> MUM: Greg, that is not obeying. Go to time-out. You have five minutes.
>
> GREG: Okay. I'll do it now. I'll take out the rubbish.
>
> MUM: No. First you have to go to time-out. You can take out the rubbish when your time is finished.

Greg misbehaved by not taking out the rubbish when asked. Mum correctly enforced time-out. Greg tried tempting her by conceding to do what Mum asked. Now he has decided that taking out the rubbish is better than having a time-out. Too late. Do not surrender to these attempts; you will be encouraging your child to badger and plead and argue. Once a rule is broken, enforce the time-out rule.

When you use time-out for the first time, begin with one misbehaviour. Choose one misbehaviour that you want to decrease. Do not choose the most troublesome misbehaviour to start, but choose a more moderate problem. This will familiarize you and your child with time-out procedures before you attempt to tackle the big problems. Be consistent with this beginning misbehaviour. Your success here sets the pattern.

When you have the first misbehaviour under control, use time-out for a second misbehaviour. Be cautious; you want your child to be successful. Moving ahead slowly is much safer than moving too quickly. Add new priority misbehaviours slowly and systematically to ensure feelings of success.

How to Explain Time-Out to Your Children

Sit down with each child separately and explain time-outs. Timing and judgement are critical; choose a time when things are going well. Do not try to explain time-out shortly after a blow-up, when you or your child is angry. Explain that a time-out is something that is going to help him behave and make better decisions. Describe time-outs as time sitting alone in the bathroom (or whatever room you are going to use). Explain how the time works – five minutes if he co-operates, longer if there is a problem. The timer will tell your child when time-out is over. If you suspect that your child may be unco-operative, explain the consequences of these actions in more detail. Finally, describe the priority misbehaviour to your child. Discuss this thoroughly and give examples. Be sure he understands the misbehaviour.

It is important to ignore any negative remarks that your child may make while you are explaining time-out. Don't expect enthusiasm. Simply explain time-out as specifically and as clearly as possible. Here is an example of a father and mother explaining time-out to their seven-year-old son.

DAD: Greg, could you come here, please? Mum and I would like to talk with you about something.

GREG: What do you want?

MUM: You have been doing pretty well with your behaviour lately in most things, but there are still times when you do not do what you are told.

DAD: We want to tell you about something that is going to help you behave and make better decisions about your behaviour.

GREG: What is it?

MUM: It's called time-out.

DAD: Time-out means going to the bathroom and sitting by yourself. If you go right away and you do not argue, you only have to sit for five minutes.

GREG: What if I don't go?

MUM: If you argue or don't go right away, then you will have to sit for ten minutes.

DAD: If you yell, or kick, or slam the bathroom door, then you will add five more minutes.

GREG: Get real. I'll be in there until I'm ten.

DAD: Do you have any questions so far?

GREG: What a stupid idea. It will never work for me. I'm too stubborn. Isn't that what you have been telling me?

DAD: When you go to time-out, we will set the timer on the oven for five minutes. When you hear the buzzer, you can come out.

MUM: But if you are noisy in there, or if you choose to have a tantrum in there, the time will not count. We will not start the timer until you are sitting quietly.

DAD: So the sooner you sit quietly, the sooner you get out.

MUM: Do you understand how the timer works?

GREG: Yes. But I still don't think it will work.

MUM: If you make a mess in the bathroom, you will have to sit an extra five minutes. You will have to clean it up before you can come out. If you break anything in there, you will have to pay for it out of your pocket money.

DAD: You will go to time-out when you do not do what we ask. When you do not obey us.

MUM: From now on, when we ask you to do something and you don't do it, you will go to time-out.

DAD: We hope that you won't have to go in there very often, but the choice is yours. If you obey, you won't need to go in there. It is really up to you.

Write down what you are going to say to your child. Make a list of things you want to discuss ahead of time. Here is an outline that will help you stay on track when explaining time-out to your child.

Explain these points:

Time-out is going to help improve behaviour.

What time-out is.

How the time works.

The use of the timer.

Describe and give an example of the priority misbehaviour.

You must remember to:

Choose a good time to talk.

Ignore any negative comments from your child.

Stay calm no matter what happens.

What to Say When Time-Out Is Over

For most misbehaviours, start fresh when your child completes time-out. If your daughter went to time-out for swearing, change the subject when she exits. Do not lecture her on the evils of using improper language. Your words are likely to land on deaf ears. The time to explain right and wrong is later, when your daughter is more receptive.

Here is an example:

SARAH: (Says a bad word)

MUM: Sarah, that's swearing. Go to time-out.

(Five minutes later, Sarah comes out of time-out.)
MUM: Have you seen my calculator anywhere?
(Mum changes the subject – to start fresh.)

Here is what NOT to do:

(Sarah comes out of time-out.)
MUM: Now aren't you sorry you said that word?
SARAH: No!
MUM: Then you march right back into time-out
        and do not come out until you are sorry!

If your child went to time-out for refusing to do something, then he must do the task when he comes out of time-out. If your son went to time-out for refusing to set the table, he must set the table when he comes out. If he refuses, send him back to time-out. Doing time-out is not a trade-in for setting the table. Do not let his refusal to set the table delay dinner; that would give him power. If you suspect that your son may not co-operate, ask him to set the table an hour before dinnertime. This gives him plenty of chances to set the table. Spending an entire hour in time-out (five minutes at a time) may encourage him to be more co-operative.

Here is a caution about time-out and chores. Having household jobs teaches children responsibility. Jobs give children an opportunity to accomplish something and feel proud (see chapter 28.) I have known some parents who expect their children to do several hours of housework every day. Children resent working if it becomes burdensome. Children need responsibilities, but they also need to be children. They should not spend hours each day doing housework. Do not use time-outs to make servants of your children.

You Can't Win If You Don't Keep Score

Keep a record or chart of your child's time-outs. Charting helps you be consistent. It is easy to be consistent with a new idea, just as it is easy to diet for three days. As the novelty wears off, we get lazy. Charting makes you stay consistent. The chart will show that your child goes to time-out less and less. Looking at the chart will make you and your child feel successful, and feeling successful will keep both of you motivated. You and your child will be achieving your goal. A sample chart appears at the end of this chapter.

Count the number of time-outs per day or per week. If the number of time-outs goes down, the system is working well. Do not be discouraged if your child's chart does not show improvement quickly; some children need more time. Some children are persistent and resist change. Some children have several good days and then a few bad days. Some children may even misbehave more at first. They want you to think that no matter what you try to do, it won't work. They think, 'I'll show you.'

Charting is important because the rate of improvement varies from child to child. Some children improve dramatically in less than a week. If this happens to your child, you will believe that time-out works well. Some children are more persistent in their misbehaviour. Improvement is much slower and more difficult to see on a day-to-day basis. It may take several weeks before you see significant improvement. You will be tempted to stop using time-out and add it to the 'We have tried everything' list. Your child may average four time-outs a day the first week. At the end of two weeks, he may average three time-outs a day. This is a small improvement. A chart will show small improvements. A chart will keep you from being discouraged if large improvements do not occur right away. There will be days when you will need all the encouragement you can get.

Many days may pass with no time-outs. Then several time-outs will occur within a few days. Some children test more than others. Every once in a while, your child will test you to see if anything has changed. He needs assurance that you still mean what you say. Charting will let you know if this happens with your child.

Sometimes time-outs increase because you are having bad days. Maybe you have let your children get away with a bit more misbehaviour than usual. You have not been as consistent as you need to be. Maybe your focus is negative. Perhaps you have forgotten to look for good behaviour.

'Go Ahead, I Like Time-Out'

What if your child says, 'Go ahead. I like time-out. It gives me a chance to get away from the rest of this crazy family for a few minutes'? Many clever children make statements like this. It may be true – at least the part about getting a break from the rest of the family – but ignore these remarks completely. This will not be easy. Do not start lecturing and moralizing. Do not respond with, 'There must be something wrong with you if you like time-out.' This will only convince your child that your button is being pushed. Do not get trapped into believing everything your child says. If you want to evaluate time-out, do not ask your child. Look at the time-out chart.

What If There Is No Improvement?

It only means there is no improvement – yet. For most parents, the reason time-out does not work is because they are too impatient. We want quicker results for our hard work. Children learn to be more persistent than their parents. Children know that if they are stubborn long enough, Mum and Dad will give in, just like all the other times.

Keep charts on time-outs for several weeks. With some children, a little improvement is all you get at first. Ask yourself these questions:

Am I being consistent? Am I following through every time the priority misbehaviour occurs? You cannot skip a few times. If you only follow through when you feel like it, you will make the problem worse. You will be teaching your child that being persistent in a negative way pays off.

Am I getting angry when I use time-out? Some children

want you to get angry. This is their goal. They will gladly serve several time-outs as long as they can push your button each time. Getting you angry may be a bigger reward than any amount of time-out. In other words, the punishment of time-out is outweighed by the reward of your anger.

Am I giving my child too much attention when I use time-out? Do not engage in long discussions and explanations. Do not let time-outs pull you away from other children or other responsibilities for long talks. Five minutes in time-out is a good trade for some of Mum's or Dad's individual attention. If time-out seems more like a game than a punishment, you are giving too much attention.

Am I forgetting to be positive about good behaviour? You cannot use time-out alone and expect it to work. Use time-outs as part of a total plan. Spend more energy on the positive than the negative. If you only concentrate on misbehaviour, time-out will not be as effective.

A parent recently told me that time-out changed her entire family. For years, she and her husband would yell and spank. The children would yell in return. Her seven-year-old son summed it up best: 'I like time-out, Mum. It's better than what we used to do.'

Time-out is a mild form of punishment that works. Use time-out with determination and planning, and arrange it in advance. This will teach your children how to predict the consequences of their behaviour and make better decisions. Use time-out consistently each time the priority misbehaviour occurs. Be calm and in control of the situation when you use time-out. If you get angry, you are using time-out incorrectly.

Your Turn

Be specific when you think about priority misbehaviours. Being specific helps you focus. This exercise will help you practise being specific. Check off the box in front of the statements that describe a specific misbehaviour.

❑ **1.** Mark hits his sister.
❑ **2.** Sarah refuses to do the dishes.
❑ **3.** Ed is obnoxious.
❑ **4.** Joe is hyperactive.
❑ **5.** Billy is running through the house.
❑ **6.** Sue nags her brother.
❑ **7.** Mary argues when you ask her to do something.

Answers: 1, 2, 5, 6 and 7 are specific. Number 3 is not specific because of the word *obnoxious*. It does not describe the misbehaviour in a meaningful way. This is also true for number 4. *Hyperactive* does not tell us exactly what Joe does when he misbehaves.

Suppose you planned to use time-out for Mark, Sarah, Billy, Sue and Mary. How would you use positive feedback to strengthen an opposite, positive behaviour for each of these children?

MARK: Compliment him when he plays nicely with his sister.

SARAH: Look for completed work. Thank her for doing her jobs.

BILLY: Compliment him when he walks calmly through the house.

SUE: Catch her saying something pleasant to her brother.

MARY: When she does something without an argument, draw her attention to it: 'Thanks for setting the table without an argument.'

Time-Out Chart

Child's Name _____

Date	Start time	End time	Misbehaviour	Comments

Use this chart to keep a record of your child's time-outs. Each time he receives a time-out, record the date, the time he went to time-out (Start time), and the time he came out of time-out (End time). Record the misbehaviour and any comments. For example:

Date	Start time	End time	Misbehaviour	Comments
6/20	12:35	12:40	Not listening	Okay!
6/20	5:45	5:55	Not listening	Argued — extra 5 min.
6/21	10:25	10:30	Not listening	Went right away

Chapter 20
How to Manage a Child Who Refuses to Go to Time-Out

The way you manage a child who refuses to go to time-out depends on the age and size of your child. For children up to five or six, it is acceptable to pick them up and put them in time-out. Be careful not to hurt your child or yourself. If your child will not stay in time-out, hold the door closed from the outside. Some parents have to do this at first.

Holding a door closed is an intense physical drain. You may feel terrible. Both parents should take turns or have another adult nearby to call on for assistance. It makes more sense to hold the door closed for a few minutes than to give in. While you are holding the door closed, it is essential that you remain calm, in control of yourself and the situation. Occasionally remind your child with a calm voice, 'As soon as you sit quietly,

I will start the timer.' If you are uncomfortable with this technique, try the next idea.

With older children or younger children who are too strong to control physically, you need a different approach. When your child refuses to go to time-out, wait a minute and ask again. If you are finding yourself getting angry, walk away and cool off for a few minutes. Do not argue or yell.

Give Your Child a Minute to Think

It is all right to give your child a minute to think about what is going to happen next. 'Before this goes any further, think about what it will mean. You are going to lose your bike. You will still have to serve your time-out. I am not going to argue with you. It's up to you. Why not do your time and get it over?' Sometimes children make poor decisions. Give them a minute to think. They may realize that ten minutes in time-out is better than a long hassle.

Take Away the Treasure

If your child refuses to go to time-out after your second request, it's time to go for something treasured. Take away the privilege or activity or toy that is most loved by your child. If possible, choose something that you can lock up or put away. Things like bicycles, CD players, computers, video games, televisions, stereos and videos work well. I do not know what your child's favourite plaything is, but you do. Whatever it is, that's what you lock up. The treasure goes to time-out.

If your son treasures riding his bicycle, and he refuses to go to time-out, lock up his bicycle. Keep it locked until he completes his ten minutes of time-out. (Add five minutes to the original five minutes because he did not co-operate.)

Some children will push you to the limit every time, hoping you will give in. They will never go to time-out until you go for the bicycle. By the time you lock up the bicycle, they have done the ten minutes. Then you have to go unlock the bicycle. You can be manipulated by this type of arrangement. If you have a loophole in your plan, your children will find it.

You can correct this situation by keeping the bicycle locked until twenty-four hours after your child serves the time-out. If your child starts the time-out when you lock up the bicycle, return the bicycle in twenty-four hours and ten minutes. If your child waits two hours to serve time-out, return the bicycle twenty-four hours after that. You may have to add that he is on full restriction until he regains his bicycle.

This back-up strategy works well. Do everything you can (except argue and get angry) to convince your child that serving five or ten minutes is better than losing his bicycle for a day. Once you start taking privileges away, the misbehaviour may escalate because your child wants to get even.

If you anticipate that your child may refuse to go to time-out, then discuss the back-up procedures when you first explain time-out.

GREG: What are you going to do if I won't go to time-out?

DAD: We will lock up your bicycle. You will get your bicycle back when you do your time-out.

MUM: If that doesn't convince you, then we will have to do something else, like locking up your bicycle for a whole day.

GREG: But that's not fair.

DAD: Well, Greg, as I said before, the choice is yours. We hope we never have to lock up your bicycle. We hope it never happens. But that is what we will do if we have to. That's a promise.

Whatever backup plan you come up with, be sure that your child's refusal to go to time-out costs your child an inconvenience, not you. Do not threaten back-up punishments that cost you more than they cost your child. Do not say, 'We cannot go out for dinner until you do your time-out.' This gives your child control over you and the entire family.

Many parents are confused about taking a privilege away as a back-up for time-out. Why not lock up the bicycle from the beginning and forget time-out? Time-out is something that is short and easy to administer. It is something that makes punishment easier for you in the long run. Time-out is easier than locking up the bicycle several times a week. If you take too many privileges away, your child may become discouraged and then give up trying to improve his behaviour.

Chapter 21
How to Be Creative with Time-Out

You forgot to set the alarm. You were going to iron in the morning. Cheers for the wrinkled look. Everyone gets bread and butter; the toaster is too slow. You say a little prayer that the car co-operates today. Do you ever start your day this way?

Why do children pick these mornings to be irritating and oppositional? Children are opportunists. They like taking advantage of stressful situations. They like to test you when you are rushed. They like to test you when you are on the phone, at church or at Grandma's. They like testing you when you have company.

Children know when time-out is difficult to enforce. They have a sixth sense about this. Children seem to misbehave when there is no time or place for time-out. Using time-out in these predicaments would be more of an inconvenience to you.

If your child misbehaves but you must be off to work, use delayed time-out. Tell your child that he will have to serve time-out later that afternoon. Remember to follow through. Write it down on your to-do list. Use delayed time-out for any inconvenient situation.

The same strategy applies when you ask your child to do something and later that day you notice that it was not done. He should go to time-out and then do what you asked earlier. Your child will resist. 'I'll vacuum the carpet now.' You may be tempted to let your child do the task and forget time-out. That would be inconsistent.

Time-Out Away from Home

Discipline begins at home. If you are positive and consistent, your child's behaviour will improve. It will improve at home, and everywhere – but not overnight. Gradually things will get better. Teach your children that you mean what you say. If you have not taught your children this at home, do not try to teach them at the grocers' shop.

Is there anything you can do at the supermarket? One alternative is to stop your shopping and return home. Send your child to time-out. Then you both return to the supermarket and try again. Some parents have done this. It sounds crazy, but the chances are you will only have to do it once. It is time-consuming, but it works well, especially with young children.

An alternative would be to use the car or car seat. Mum took Josh, three, to the bank. It was Friday, and the queues were long and slow. Josh decided to misbehave. Mum got out of line and took him to his car seat. He sat there for two minutes while Mum stood behind the car, watching him. He settled down, and they returned to the bank. This is a good example of consistency. Mum knew it was worth it to teach Josh that misbehaving is not permitted. She was thinking about the future.

Establish a time-out setting at places you visit regularly. Use the bathroom at Grandma's. Use the laundry room at Diane's house. Another alternative is to promise time-out when you get home. Do not threaten your child with time-out. Promise time-out. Children know that threats are meaningless. A promise is a commitment. You must follow through with time-out when you get home. If you are consistent with time-out at home and in public, your child's behaviour will improve.

Time-Out for Two

What should you do when two (or more) of your children misbehave at the same time? It is best to avoid discussions about who started it. This usually leads to more arguing and more disagreement. If both children have misbehaved, then both should go to time-out – but not together. One child sits while the other does time-out, and then they trade places. Flip a coin to see who goes first.

Time-Out for Tiny Tots

Leah's first exposure to time-out occurred when she was about a year old. Leah toddled up to play with the TV. I picked her up and put her in the playpen, which was empty and in another room. I said, 'No TV.' I stood there for about thirty seconds and then took her out of the playpen. I said, 'No TV,' and put her down on the floor.

Naturally, she darted for the TV, so I repeated the same procedure. Into the playpen she went. I said, 'No TV.' When she got out, she crawled nonstop for the TV. It took five repetitions, but she finally stopped. It wasn't the last time she tried playing with the TV. Every time she tried, she found herself in the playpen. We were very consistent about this.

We were teaching Leah not to play with the TV. We were also teaching her something more important. We were teaching the meaning of the word *No*. We were laying the foundation for our parental authority.

You can use time-out with children between the ages of one

and two years. But be cautious; children at this age do not fully understand language. They are naturally curious, have an abundance of energy, and do not like to stay in one place. Their attention span is only a few seconds long. They are easily upset and they cry a lot. They have a knack for getting into trouble. They do not realize that putting a fork into an electric socket is a bad idea. Children at this age do not know right from wrong. Do not think of their actions as misbehaviour.

Use time-out to teach young children what is acceptable and what is not acceptable. Use time-out to teach what is safe and what is not safe. Use time-out to teach toddlers that screaming to get what they want is not appropriate. You can also use time-out to teach them not to do certain things, like playing with the television.

Some parents have asked about using a crib for time-out with infants. Cribs are supposed to be a place for comfort and sleep. Using a crib for time-out would cause the infant to associate his crib with displeasure.

For young children, use an empty playpen for time-out. Do not give away your playpen if your infant has outgrown it. Now it has another use. Many parents purchase a second playpen – one for toys, one to use for time-out. You may want to put the playpen in a spare room. When you put your child in time-out, always stand nearby. Time-out should last between thirty seconds and one minute. Whenever possible, tell your child what he is doing that you do not like. Keep it simple, such as 'No TV' or 'No plugs' or 'No crayons on the wall.'

Manage tantrums differently. If your child is having a tantrum because he wants a biscuit, you may want to leave your child in the playpen until the screaming stops. You may need to walk away, just out of his field of view, before he will stop. Peep at him every few seconds. The moment the crying stops, take your child out of the playpen. Say, 'You stopped crying. Good for you.' Redirect his tantrum. 'It's hard for me to listen to whining. How do you ask for a biscuit?' If he does not stop crying after two or three minutes, pick him up and redirect him anyway.

Time-Out Guidelines

Determine the time-out setting
>   Safety first
>   As boring as possible

Identify one priority misbehaviour
Use a timer
>   Explain time-out to your child
>   Time-out is going to improve behaviour
>   What time-out is
>   How the time works
>   How the timer works
>   Describe the priority misbehaviour (give an example)

Use time-out as part of a plan
Be consistent with time-out
Stay calm when you use time-out
Use a chart to keep a record of progress
Initial episodes may be difficult (extinction burst)

The time in time-out

>   5 minutes if you co-operate
>   10 minutes if you do not

Start the time when your child is sitting quietly (a little crying is okay)

The child who refuses to go

Put little ones in
Take away the treasure
>   until the time-out is done
>   until the time-out is done plus 24 hours
>   (or a reasonable added time)

When your child completes time-out

Start fresh – redirect (if the misbehaviour is over)
>   *or*

Your child still has to do what is asked (if he went to
   time-out for refusing a request)

Use delayed time-out

>   For inconvenient times
>   When away from home

Time-out for two: flip a coin and take turns.

Chapter 22

How to Manage Arguments and Power Struggles

'Can I spend the night at Corey's house?'

'Not tonight, I'd like you to stay at home with us.'

'I haven't gone to Corey's for over a month.'

'Not tonight, please.'

'There's nothing to do here. It's boring.'

'Please don't argue.'

'I don't get it. Why can't I go? Give me one good reason.'

'Because I said so. If you don't stop arguing, you are going to be grounded.'

'Big deal. Go ahead and ground me. What's the difference? I can't ever do anything anyway.'

'Okay. You're grounded for the entire weekend. Go to your room.'

'I can't wait until I grow up and get out of this house.'

Children love to argue. They want their ideas to be everyone else's ideas. They like to prove that they are right and you and everyone else are wrong. Children like to control the situation. They enjoy having power over their parents.

Children have a need for power. Ths need is normal; children see adults as having power. We do what we want to do; at least, that's what our children think. We appear self-reliant and secure. We are all grown up. We have power. Children want to be like us. They want power too.

Having a need for power is not a bad thing. It is only when a child uses power in a negative way that power can become a problem. Power-seeking children try to do what they want to do. They refuse to do what you ask. Children who seek power do not like to be told what to do. They resist authority. They like to make the rules. They like to determine how things are going to be done.

Why You Can't Win a Power Struggle

Most parents deal with power by emphasizing countercontrol. This does not work. Efforts to control a power-seeking child often lead to a deadlock or power struggle between your child and you. No final victory is ever possible for you. Once you find yourself in a power struggle, you have lost.

If your child wins the power struggle, he is reassured that power caused the victory. You were defeated by his power. If you win the power struggle, your child thinks that it was your power that caused the victory and defeated him. He is reassured of the value of power. This results in children striking back, again and again, each time with stronger methods. You win the battle but lose the war.

Every child displays power differently. Most power struggles are active. Arguing is a good example of active power. Some children have learned the value of passive resistance. Rather than argue, these children will refuse to do what you ask. They nod their heads and just sit quietly. Some even smile a little.

This type of power has a definite purpose – to push your buttons.

How to Handle Power

Stop being part of the power struggle. It takes two to have a power struggle. It takes two to argue. Make a firm commitment to yourself that you will no longer engage in arguments and lengthy explanations. State your expectations clearly and firmly and walk away. Tell your child exactly what you want him to do, when he must do it, and what happens if he does not. Then walk away.

> 'It's time to turn off the TV.'
> 'I want to watch the next show.'
> 'Sorry, it's time to get ready for bed.'
> 'Can't I stay up for one more show?'
> 'Not tonight. We have to get up early.'
> 'We always have to get up early.'
> 'Turn off the TV. Have your shower and go to bed.
>   Do it now, or you will lose TV for tomorrow
>   night.'

Do not stay in the situation and argue. Go to your room and close the door if necessary. Do not let your child push your buttons. If you get angry, you will be rewarding your child. Your anger will give your child the power over you that he seeks. You may need to use punishment when dealing with power. Tell your child what to do. Be ready with a punishment if your child fails to co-operate. If you punish a child because of a power struggle, remember two things. First, do not punish in anger; this will only encourage your child to strike back with power. Second, smaller punishments work better than bigger punishments. If your child thinks you have punished him too harshly, he will retaliate with power.

When your child does what you ask without an argument, thank him. Call attention to it: 'Thank you. You did what I asked without an argument. I appreciate that. It shows you are co-operating.' As a long-term solution, remember that a child's need for power can be a positive thing. Look for independence, self-reliance, leadership and decision making. When your child shows these qualities, spotlight them. Catch him being good. As with most behaviour problems, the positive approach is the best remedy for handling power.

The Difference Between Power and Authority

The difference between power and authority lies within you. When you have to confront your children, emphasize co-operation, not control. Stay calm and rational in spite of the situation. Guard your anger button. Stop and think. Do not react impulsively. Give clear and specific expectations. Explain what will happen if your child chooses not to co-operate. Do not give ultimatums. Focus on influencing your child's motivation.

Here is an example of a parent using power:

'Why can't I go?'
'Because I said so. I'm your father.'
'What has that got to do with it?'
'Everything.'
'Well, I'm going anyway.'
(Dad gets angry.) 'I'm warning you. If you go to that party, you are going to be in big trouble.'
'Oh sure. What are you going to do?'
'You just wait and see.'

Here is an example of a parent using authority:

'Why can't I go?'
'I don't think it is going to be safe.'
'I can handle it.'

'There is going to be a lot of drinking at that party.
Probably drugs too. I don't want you there.'

'I'll be okay. You don't have to worry.'

'You don't understand. I trust you. That's not the
problem. I don't trust some of those other kids.
You can't control what they will do.'

'Everyone else is going.'

'I know you want to go very much. I know you'll
be disappointed.'

'I want to go.'

'Sorry. You can't go. You can do something else.
Ask some friends over here.'

How to Correct Your Child Without an Argument

Giving verbal corrections is difficult. Verbal correction can turn
into arguments, especially if you get angry. Yelling, scolding and
threatening help you vent your anger, but they do not correct
misbehaviour. Sometimes they make the misbehaviour worse.

Stay calm. Tell your children to stop. Be ready to enforce a
punishment if you must. Do not become caught in the cycle of
yelling and threatening. You do not want to spend the rest of
your life that way. Getting angry and yelling makes arguments
worse. If your child's goal is to push your buttons and get
you angry, yelling is a reward for misbehaving. Yelling will
strengthen unwanted behaviour.

How can you correct your children and avoid arguments?
Verbal corrections are part of good discipline. The purpose of
verbal corrections is to teach better decision making. Here are
some suggestions.

1. Begin by validating your relationship: 'You are my son and
   I love you. Nothing you do will ever change that.'
2. State your concern: 'Your behaviour at the shop was not
   acceptable. I was embarrassed.'

3. Remind your child of previous good behaviour: 'That's not like you. You are always very well behaved when we go shopping.'

4. Separate your child from his behaviour. Say, 'That behaviour is unacceptable.' Do not say, 'Anyone who would do that is stupid.'

5. React appropriately to the size of the problem. If your child misbehaves while shopping, restrict him from shopping: 'You can't go shopping with me for two weeks. You will have to stay at home. I hope that when you can come with me again, you will behave.'

Do not ask why. Children misbehave because they choose to misbehave. When you ask why, you are suggesting there may be an excuse: 'Why did you do that?' 'He told me to do it.' Clever children will search for excuses until they come up with one that you accept. If you don't accept it, you then have a power struggle on your hands.

Realize that an upset child is not a good listener. This is not the time for constructive communication. Wait until he cools off.

Teach your children to learn from their mistakes rather than suffer from them. Point out things they do wrong by showing them ways to do it better: 'You remembered to take out the rubbish. Good going. The twist ties need to be a little tighter next time. I'll show you how.'

Admit you are wrong once in a while. This is a tough one. Your children will learn from your example. When you openly admit your mistakes and weaknesses, you are showing them that grown-ups are not perfect. We don't know everything. Anthony attended a meeting I had with a proofreader of this book. He could not believe that she had so many suggestions. It was good for him to see that his dad is not perfect. It was also good for him to see that I did not take the corrections personally. I explained that she was helping me make the book better. I showed him that it's okay to make errors.

Do not carry on about small mistakes; deal with them and then let them go. The purpose of verbal corrections is to have a more co-operative youngster. Misbehaviours and mistakes are normal. You can help your child best by minimizing problems. Do not dwell on them, or rehash the day's problems with your spouse in front of your child. Children cannot build on weaknesses. They can only build on strengths.

These same ideas apply when your children are arguing with each other. Stay calm and do not make threats. If you can, help your children reach a settlement. Brandon and Marie have been arguing for ten minutes. Dad has had enough. Finally, he gets angry. He yells, 'Stop or you will both go to bed.'

Most children will be quiet for a while when threatened. Unfortunately, Dad thinks that yelling works. This is a mistake. Yelling works temporarily, but the quiet will not last. Yelling and threatening have no long-term effect on misbehaviour. The children argue; Dad yells; they quieten down for a while. Soon, they argue again. Dad yells. They quieten down again. This can go on and on. These children will learn that they can argue until Dad yells at them to stop. They will not learn to solve their problems.

A little humour may help. Here is a way to neutralize arguments in the car. Whenever you are on a trip and the children start to argue, ask them to stop. If they don't stop, begin talking about a trip for parents only. 'This explains why so many parents leave their children at home. Next trip, let's go somewhere romantic.' When children hear this, they get the point.

When Children Get Even

When a child feels hurt or angry, he may want to get even. He wants to hurt you. Getting even takes away some of his hurt and anger. Getting even makes children feel that justice has been served. Revenge is important to children because of their keen sense of fairness.

Revenge can destroy relationships between parents and children. This is especially true of teenagers. Some children embarrass you in front of others. Some children strike out at something that is special to you. Some children hurt a younger brother or sister. Some children run away. Some children will break a window or break something of value. I once worked with a mother who had a vengeful teenage son. One day she came home to find that he had thrown all of her fine china and crystal glasses into the street. Revenge is not pleasant.

Revenge typically begins when you punish your child for something he believes is unfair. He decides to get even with you by misbehaving again. He pushes your buttons. You get angry and punish again. He strikes back again. The cycle of retaliation begins.

Breaking the Cycle of Retaliation

The target of your child's revenge is your feelings. A child who wants to get even wants to hurt you. If he does, he has achieved his payoff. Some parents lack self-confidence about their skills as a parent. Clever children realize this and take full advantage of the parent's weakness.

Revenge-seeking children know exactly where to strike. They say things such as, 'I hate you. You're a terrible mother.' The reason for these remarks is to make you feel hurt. You feel that you have failed your children. They want you to feel inadequate and guilty.

When you feel inadequate or guilty, you begin to question your own judgments. *Then you begin to give in.* There is nothing a revenge-seeking child would like more than for you to become inconsistent. This is the payoff they are looking for.

Believe in your own abilities and you will not become the victim of your child's revenge. Support yourself. When your child strikes at your buttons, remain strong. Tell yourself that you are a good parent – you are doing the best you can.

Be positive when disciplining your children. Do not criticize. Be sure that punishments are fair and that they make sense to your child. Punishments should not humiliate or embarrass your child. Punishments should be mild. They should teach your child to make better decisions. Do not use punishment to get even with your child for something he has done that hurts you or makes you angry.

Control yourself. Do not let him push your buttons. Have faith in your judgment. Do not give in to arguments like: 'Taylor's mum lets him watch X-rated movies.' Do not reward your child's revenge. The more confidence you have, the easier it will be for you to win your child's co-operation.

Many parents measure their worthiness by their children's success: 'If I am a good parent, why are my kids so bad?' They feel that if their children are not perfect, then they must be less than adequate as parents. By believing this, you are making yourself vulnerable to your children. You become an easy target for any child looking for a button to push.

Think about the reasons you might feel this way. Are you insecure about yourself? Do you feel this way because of your spouse? Is this a leftover belief from your relationship with your parents? Think about your strengths rather than your insecurities. The more you focus on your strengths, the more confident you will become. Stay calm when your child says, 'I hate you.' Say, 'I'm sorry you feel that way, but I have to do what's right.'

Being a good parent does not always mean that you will be your child's best friend. There have been times when my children have been angry at me. I do not like how it feels, yet I am not going to give in to their demands. I am not going to criticize myself. Ten years from now they will not remember the time I would not let them watch an X-rated movie. But they will remember my commitment to them. I am going to support myself because I know that what I am doing is best.

Your Turn

Robert is an active ten-year-old. He is not a malicious child, but he is usually in one kind of trouble or another. His parents love him very much, but they are fed up with his misbehaviour. They try to be positive, but sometimes they forget. Dad does the punishing. He says he has tried 'everything', even time-out on a few occasions. When asked about Robert, Dad replies that he is always in trouble: 'He gets so obnoxious I could scream. I've tried it all. We just go around in circles and argue. You should see how he treats his mother. The only thing that stops him is the paddle. I spend half my life hitting that kid. You think he would learn. It seems that every time I think about it, he is doing something to upset me. I won't give up. I'll make him behave or else.' What could these parents be doing differently? Make a list of your ideas and suggestions.

Here are some ideas.

1. Robert's parents need to change their behaviour first. They are trapped by Robert's misbehaviour. That's all they see. He is 'always' in trouble. He gets so 'obnoxious'. They need to be more specific. They need to look for opposite, positive behaviour, such as doing what he is asked without an argument.

2. 'Dad does the punishing.' Mum and Dad need to work together, or Robert will manipulate and continue to mistreat Mum.

3. They have tried 'everything'. Robert is a persistent child. He has learned that he can outlast anything his parents try. Mum and Dad need to be more patient. They need to stick with one strategy. You cannot use time-out on a few occasions. You must use it consistently.

4. Mum and Dad need to stop arguing with Robert. Dad should give up the 'behave or else' attitude, which only creates more resistance in Robert. They need to tell Robert what he must do, when he must do it, what happens if he does, and what happens if he does not. Then they must calmly follow through.

5. Dad believes that spanking stops Robert. It does not. Robert does not behave to avoid the spanking. Spankings have not changed Robert's behaviour. Try a punishment that does not provoke Robert to the point of retaliation.

Here is a chart that summarizes the difference between power and authority.

Power	Authority
Emphasize **co-operation,**	not **control.**
Stay **rational,**	not **emotional.**
Keep your **self-control;**	do not get **angry.**
Stop and **think;**	do not act **impulsively.**
Be **proactive;**	not **reactive.**
Relate consequences to behaviour and choices;	do not give **ultimatums.**
Remain **child centred,**	not **self-centred.**

Chapter 23
Reducing Attention Seeking

'Mummy, come here and see my picture.'
'It's very nice, Sarah.'
'I can't find the blue crayon.'
'It's right here.'
'I can't find the green one.'
'Here it is.'
'I don't want to colour. I want to paint.'
'I'll get your paint set.'
'Will you paint this flower for me, Mummy?'

It's normal for children to need attention and approval. However, attention-seeking becomes a problem when it happens all the time. Even charming attention-seeking can become controlling. Many children make tragedies out of trivial concerns to get your sympathy. Excessive attention-seeking results in a situation where your child commands your life.

Many children misbehave to get attention. The most notorious reason for misbehaviour in young children, this can be the seed for discipline problems in later childhood and adolescence.

Your goal is not to eliminate your child's need for attention and approval. When handled correctly, your child's need for attention can be a helpful tool for improving your child's behaviour. Eliminate not the need for attention, but the attention-seeking behaviour that is excessive or unacceptable. A mother who says, 'Sarah, I know that you want me to stay and paint with you. I'm busy now. If you can be patient and paint by yourself for ten minutes, I'll be able to spend some time with you then,' is giving Sarah an opportunity to have the attention that she wants and needs. She is not giving in to nagging.

How Much Attention Is Too Much?

That depends on you. How much attention-seeking can you tolerate? The rule is that children will seek as much attention as you give them. You must strike a balance between how much your children want and how much you can give. Even normal attention-seeking can drive you crazy on some days.

Do not let your children's need for attention turn into demands for attention. When children do not get enough attention, they resort to outbursts, tantrums, nagging, badgering and other annoying behaviours. They think, if I can't get attention by being good, then I'll misbehave to get Mum's attention.

Three Kinds of Attention

Adult attention and approval are among the strongest rewards for children. Unfortunately, parents seldom use attention wisely. There are three kinds of attention:

Positive Attention
Negative Attention
No Attention

When you give your children attention and approval for being well behaved, they are getting positive attention. Positive attention means catching children being good. Focus on positive behaviour. Positive attention can be words of praise or encouragement, closeness, hugs or a pat on the back. A friendly note in your child's lunch box works well. Positive attention increases good behaviour.

When you give your child attention for misbehaviour, you are giving negative attention. Negative attention typically begins when you become upset. You follow with threats, interrogation and lectures. Negative attention is not a punishment, it is a reward. Negative attention does not punish misbehaviour, but increases it.

What is the easiest way to capture your attention – sitting quietly or misbehaving? When children do not receive attention in a positive way, they will get your attention any way they can. Do not pay attention to misbehaviours. Pay attention to good behaviour. Avoid this scenario:

> Jeremy and Dominic are sitting quietly and watching Saturday morning cartoons for thirty minutes. Everything is peaceful. Dad is working on the computer. Suddenly, an argument erupts: 'It's my turn to pick a show.' Dad charges into the room. He turns off the television, scolds the two children, and sends them to their rooms.

For thirty minutes, these children were well behaved. Dad said nothing to them about how well they were doing. Nothing was said about how quiet they were. Nothing was said about how well they were co-operating. The moment there was trouble, Dad was instantly mobilized. Dad did not give them any positive attention while they were being good. When they began misbehaving, Dad rushed in with plenty of negative attention.

Negative attention teaches children how to manipulate and get their way. They learn to be troublesome. They learn how to interrupt you. They learn how to control you. Negative attention teaches children how to badger, nag and annoy. It teaches children to aggravate, irritate and exasperate. We teach this by not paying attention to our children when they are behaving appropriately, and by paying attention to them when they are misbehaving.

I have worked with hundreds of parents who have taught their children to be negative attention seekers. I have never met a parent who taught this deliberately. When you attend to the negative and ignore the positive, you teach your children to behave in a negative way. Your child will misbehave to get your attention in the future.

Do not wait for misbehaviour to happen. Do not take good behaviour for granted. We do this with teenagers. We come to expect good behaviour and overlook their efforts. When a child demonstrates good behaviour, notice it. Look for it. The more you notice, the more you will find. You will get more good behaviour in the future. Anyone can catch children being bad. Turn this around. Catch them being good. It's not easy. It takes practice.

Statistics show that the average parent spends seven minutes a week with each of their children. Do better than average. Telling your children that you love them is not enough. Show them that you love them. Spend ten minutes of quality time with each child every day. No excuses, like I was just too busy today, or I didn't have time. We are all too busy.

In many families, both parents work. Some parents have two jobs. Your most important job is being a parent. When you come home after work, give the first thirty minutes to your children. Do not be the parents whose only hour with their daughter this week was in the principal's office or at the police station. Write your children into your diary. Make an appointment with each of your children every day. Go for a walk and listen to what is happening in their lives. Turn off the TV for an hour and talk.

How to Ignore

When you ignore misbehaviour, you are giving no attention. Because attention is rewarding to children, withholding attention can be an effective punishment. Withholding attention can weaken a misbehaviour. When your child misbehaves to get your attention, ignore the misbehaviour. Ignore your child's inappropriate demands for attention. You will weaken those demands and extinguish the misbehaviour.

Some parents find this hard to believe; they think that if a child is misbehaving, he must be punished. This is not true. Ignoring demands for attention is the best cure. When you ignore consistently, you will teach your child that these misbehaviours are not paid off with attention. Temper tantrums need an audience. Take the audience away, and there is no point to having a tantrum. *Do not forget to redirect.* Teach children appropriate ways to get attention. 'My ears do not listen to whining. Please ask in a soft voice.'

When to Ignore

Ignoring does not mean ignoring the problem. It means ignoring demands for negative attention. There are many misbehaviours that you should not ignore. Some misbehaviours should be punished. Deciding when to ignore or when to punish is not easy and there are no exact rules. It takes timing and judgment. When your child misbehaves to get attention, ignore it. If your child does not stop in two or three minutes, give him a reminder. Tell your child, 'I do not respond to whining. When you stop, we'll talk.' Wait another minute or two. If he still does not stop, then tell your child to stop or he will be punished: 'Stop now, or you will go to time-out.'

If you get angry or let your child push your buttons, you lose. If you must use a punishment, dispense the punishment without anger. If you get angry, then your child has succeeded in getting the negative attention that he was after. If you feel yourself getting angry, walk away. Cool off. If you give in, you will be providing your child with an attention payoff. You will be rewarding a misbehaviour.

Do not take good behaviour for granted: give your children positive attention when they are behaving. Ignore demands for attention such as badgering and whining; giving in to these demands encourages children to misbehave to get attention. Understanding these ideas is easy, but practising them is difficult. You are worth it. Make the commitment. Your children are worth it too.

Chapter 24
What to Do About Misbehaviour

One of the most exasperating aspects of parenthood is managing misbehaviour. When our children misbehave, we often feel frustrated and discouraged. When we are caught up in the midst of a misbehaviour event, we are not always at our best. We may be angry or upset, and our use of reason often disappears. All we want is for the misbehaviour to stop – now! Wouldn't it be nice if there were a specific, effective strategy right at your fingertips? Here it is. This plan will help you determine the most effective way of managing your children's misbehaviour. The plan has three steps, and each requires a decision.

Step 1: Determine the pattern of misbehaviour.
Most acts of misconduct occur as part of a pattern. Children develop one or more patterns of misbehaviour to get what they

want or express an emotion. There are four typical patterns of misbehaviour:

* Annoying misbehaviour, such as whining, badgering, nagging, sulking or tantrums.
* Disobedient misbehaviour, such as not following rules or not doing chores.
* Aggressive misbehaviour, which can be verbal, such as name-calling or put-downs, or physical, such as biting, kicking, hitting, spitting or fighting.
* Defiant misbehaviour, such as refusing to listen or arguing.

Identifying the pattern of misbehaviour is helpful because it leads to the purpose or function of the misbehaviour.

Step 2: Decide the purpose of misbehaviour.

Although you can never be certain of the motivation or purpose of a child's misconduct, we do know that most misbehaviour does have a purpose. Once you identify the misbehaviour pattern, think about the purpose behind it.

When misbehaviour is annoying, children may be trying to get their way. They may be trying to get you to give in, or to change your mind. When children are disobedient, it may be because they are not internally or externally motivated to do what you want. They may be very motivated to do something else, like ignore you. This can be for control or power. Children who exhibit aggressive behaviour are often expressing anger, frustration or revenge. They may be hurt or angry because they did not get their way or because they believe that you have done something against them. Children who are defiant are typically after control or power. They either do not want to do what you ask or want to do what you do not permit.

Step 3: Decide what to say and do.

Since the purpose of most annoying behaviour is to get you to give in or change your mind, one correct way to manage annoying behaviour is to ignore it. This does not mean to ignore the problem. The correct action is to ignore the whining or badgering. Do not give in to demands. Tantrums need an audience. It is fine to say, 'I am ignoring you.' It is also helpful to use redirection: 'My ears do not listen to whining, please ask in a polite voice.' As a long-term solution, provide correct examples and positive reinforcement for replacement behaviour, such as asking politely and speaking calmly.

A good way to manage verbal aggression such as name-calling and swearing is to minimize their effects by not overreacting. This is often difficult. It helps to talk with your child during a calm moment and explain the consequences of name-calling – how words can hurt other's feelings: 'That is not acceptable. It is okay to be upset (angry), but it is not okay to used bad words and hurt another person's feelings.' As a long-term solution, provide correct examples and positive reinforcement for replacement behaviour, such as properly expressing anger with words or pictures.

A way to manage physical aggression such as biting, kicking, hitting, spitting or fighting is to intervene quickly and stop the aggression. Then redirect your child and explain that it is okay to be upset, but it is not okay to strike out: 'That is not acceptable. It is okay to be upset (angry), but it is not okay to hit.' For younger children, redirect with: 'Use your words.' This helps young children learn to use words to express how they feel. If there is a pattern, take more deliberate action, such as time-out. Once the child is calm and can talk, provide discussion and explanation. Always explain the consequences: someone could be hurt, either physically or emotionally. As a long-term solution, provide correct examples and positive reinforcement for replacement behaviour, such as playing together, sharing, speaking politely, and properly expressing anger with words or pictures.

Children who are defiant and refuse to listen or obey are usually after control. Remain calm. If you get upset, the child wins. This is the victory they seek. Be consistent. Be prepared to follow through the first time. As a long-term solution, provide positive reinforcement for replacement behaviour, such as listening the first time. Say, 'Thank you for listening the first time I asked you to take out the rubbish. I appreciate it very much.' It is especially important to remain calm when your children try to argue. Use redirection: 'If you speak to me calmly, I will listen to what you have to say.' If you find yourself getting sucked into an argument, remember to control yourself first. Say, 'I need to calm down before this goes any further. I am going to deal with me, and then I'll come back and deal with you.' As a long-term solution, provide reinforcement for replacement behaviour, such as listening the first time or doing what is asked without an argument.

When a child is being disobedient, give a firm warning that the behaviour must stop, or you will take action: 'Think about what you are doing. If you continue, you will be punished. You decide.' In other words, give a firm warning, point out that this behaviour is not a good idea, and explain that the child needs to make a better decision, or punishment will occur. Explain that a poor choice will result in a negative consequence or outcome, and a good choice will result in a positive consequence or outcome: 'It's okay to not want to do it – but you still have to do it.' 'There will always be things we have to do that we don't want to do.' Use yourself as an example. As a long-term solution, provide positive reinforcement for replacement behaviour, such as being obedient and respectful.

Part v

Dealing with Violence in Our Society and With Our Children

Chapter 25
How to Raise a Nonviolent Child

Whenever I am asked what is different about children today compared to thirty years ago, when I started working with children, I immediately answer, *anger*. We have so many angry children, and the degree of anger is significantly more intense. There are children who are angry every day of their lives. They wake up angry, go to school angry and go to bed angry.

Since children do not manage anger well, anger often results in conflict with siblings, peers, parents, teachers and authority figures. When conflicts are not resolved, anger can turn into aggression, revenge and violence. The way today's children react with revenge and violence is more excessive, cruel and brutal. Thirty years ago, the most violent act we would see at school would be an occasional fight, which might have resulted in a couple of black eyes. Today in America children use knives, guns and even bombs to express violence. Anger is the primary reason behind the excessive violence in our children.

A Brief Overview of Anger

Anger exists in everyone. Occasional anger is normal; chronic anger is not. Chronic anger can destroy relationships. Chronic anger can damage our mental health and our physical health. Typically, aggression, revenge and violence occur when anger becomes chronic. The purpose of this chapter is to help you teach your children how to manage their occasional anger and keep it from becoming chronic.

It is helpful to think of anger as a secondary emotion. Something will happen to upset you and then you become angry. Something happens to activate the anger. As parents, our children may disappoint or frustrate us, and we get angry. We may become angry when our children disobey, defy or talk back. A child may experience teasing, hurt, failure or rejection and become angry. Many children become angry when they do not get their way or when they believe that something is unfair. These initial, activating events are called triggers. We all have our own unique set of triggers. My anger can still be triggered when I see a child bullying a younger child.

Anger is part of our temperament – our overall mood or disposition. Temperament is inborn. Some parents have anger that is more easily triggered, and so do some children.

Anger is also learned. When children live with parents who are angry, children learn to be angry. When a child sees a parent acting out his anger by screaming or hitting, he learns that it is okay to scream and hit when you are angry.

How do so many children become angry? There are a number of factors. There are more angry adults in our world today. Road rage was unheard of thirty years ago. More angry adults means more angry children. Some children are angry because they have been excessively punished or punished unfairly. When children live in a hostile or critical home, they become angry because of feelings of despair and hopelessness. Many children are angry because of prolonged sadness or unhappiness. This can lead to depression, which is anger aimed inwards. Children are angry because of divorce. Many children of divorce become angry because they feel alone or abandoned. They do not have a solid connection with an adult or with their family.

Teaching Anger Management

Teach your children to recognize and regulate their anger. Teach them how anger affects their body. When you are angry, your heart beats faster. You may breathe hard. Your face muscles feel tight. Your eyes might squint. Your body is rigid. You may clench your fists. You may feel like screaming or hitting.

Teach your children that it is normal to feel angry, especially if someone has hurt your feelings. You may want to get even, but hitting or fighting does not solve the problem; thinking and talking are better ways. Tell your child,

> 'When you are angry with someone, you may think about hitting him. You feel that you want to hurt him because he did something to hurt you. Whenever you get even with someone because you are angry, it is not a good solution. When you are feeling angry, the best thing to do is tell someone. Tell someone you trust. Talk with your dad or me. Talk with your teacher or a good friend. When you talk about anger it helps you feel better.'

Teach your child strategies for calming and redirecting himself when he becomes angry. Choose a time when your child is quiet and receptive. Do not try to teach calming techniques when your child is in the middle of an angry outburst. Practise techniques such as deep breathing, counting to ten, playing with a favourite toy, or going to their room and taking a rest or listening to relaxing music. When your child becomes angry, use a verbal reminder or cue to help him calm down.

Jordan would often get angry when she did not get her way. Mark taught Jordan how to use deep breathing to calm down. Mark began by telling Jordan that deep breathing is an idea that many adults use to help calm down. Then he showed her what to do. He put his hand on his chest and took two deep breaths. Jordan did the same. When Mark saw Jordan getting upset, he would cue her by putting his hand on his chest and taking a deep breath. This would help Jordan remember to use deep breathing to calm down.

Wendy also taught Conner to use breathing to control his temper. She knew she was making progress when one day Conner reminded her, 'Mum, you are getting mad. Take a few deep breaths.'

Role-playing is an excellent way to practise anger management. Ask your child to think of a situation that makes him angry. Brainstorm possible solutions. Then role-play the situation. We often tell our children to walk away and ignore others who are teasing them or trying to get them angry. Walking away is not easy. It takes practice. Edward used role-playing to help Charles learn to manage his anger when his friends teased him. Edward played the role of Charles's friend Arthur.

ARTHUR : (Edward)	'What an ugly shirt. Did your sister buy you that shirt?'
CHARLES:	'I'm sorry you don't like it. I bought it, and I like it.'
ARTHUR:	'It looks like my sister's shirt.'
CHARLES:	'I like it.'
ARTHUR:	'It's ugly.'
CHARLES:	'I'm going to the playground. See you later.' (Charles walks away.)

You may need to practise role-playing several different situations. This helps children take what they learn by role-playing into the real world. Role-playing works with any age of child. Young children call it pretending. After each role-playing activity, praise your child for his effort and desire to learn to manage anger.

Teach your children to learn from their anger. Talk with your children after an anger episode. Be sure to wait long enough so that your child is ready to talk and listen. Many parents want to rush into this while the child is still angry. This could be a mistake because it could re-ignite the anger. It may be helpful to say, 'Let me know when you are ready to talk about this.'

Begin your talk by asking your child to remember what happened to get the anger started: 'What is making you upset?' With older children you may actually label this the trigger event. Then ask the child why the trigger got the anger going: 'Can you say why this upset you so much?' If your child has trouble using words to describe what happened, you might want to offer some ideas: 'It sounds like you felt left out of the game.'

In some cases, you may want to ask if the anger was helpful: 'Did getting angry help you feel better? Did getting angry change what happened?' Finally, you want to talk about alternatives: 'What else could you have done?' 'What have you done before that may have worked better?' For most children, simply talking about anger is a helpful way of learning about anger management.

DAD:	'I would like to talk about this, now.'
NICK:	'Talk about what?'
DAD:	'Talk about what happened and what made you so angry. Can you tell me what happened, please?'
NICK:	'I got mad because he took my CD without asking me.'
DAD:	'Your brother took your CD, and you got mad.'
NICK:	'Yes.'
DAD:	'I can understand that. Did getting angry help?'
NICK:	'Not really. We just got into an argument.'
DAD:	'Can you think of something else you could have said?'
NICK:	'No!'
DAD:	'I might have said, "It really upsets me when you take my stuff. Please ask me next time." Can you try that?'
NICK:	'I don't know if that will work.'
DAD:	'If you try it next time, you will know. It sounds better than fighting!'

Many children have difficulty using words to describe how they feel. Teach your children to express themselves with drawings. This helps young children get started. Once they have a picture, you can ask about events and feelings.

Susan asked Jack to pose for several pictures. In one picture he would smile, in another he would frown, in another he would make an angry face. Then Susan drew a picture of a thermometer on a large chart. She labelled the thermometer from bottom to top: calm, upset, angry, hot and steaming. She taught Jack to choose a picture that showed his feelings and then place it on the thermometer. This enabled Jack to express himself and gave Susan a tool to begin talking with Jack about his anger. Pictures and words are always better than hitting.

Older children can use a diary to help reflect on their anger. Teach them to write down what happened, how they got angry, and what they did after they got angry. This helps children see patterns to triggers and reactions.

None of these suggestions will work unless you model and practise anger management yourself. You cannot just tell your children what to do. You have to show them. You need to be a living example. Your children will learn to manage their anger by watching the way you manage your anger.

For most parents, anger habits are learned. The way you manage your anger is part of your parenting style and is sometimes affected by your temperament. Some parents suppress their anger and let it simmer until it boils over, and then explode over a little misbehaviour. This confuses children; they never know when you are going to go off. Some parents vent their anger by 'blasting' at every chance they get. This may seem to work sometimes, but the constant yelling only teaches children to stay out of your way. Children learn that yelling, screaming and adult tantrums are a way to control. None of these styles teaches your children good anger-management strategies.

Parents who are successful anger managers are good models for their children. They have learned to handle anger in a way that is constructive rather than destructive. They have learned to acknowledge their anger and then use it to solve the problem or improve the situation. Parents who manage their anger are aware of their triggers, and they plan to prevent these events from becoming button pushers.

Frustration is a common parent trigger. We work hard each day to provide our children with a fine home and a secure future, and yet the rubbish sits there for days. You might say, 'I am upset that the rubbish is still in the kitchen. I asked you to take it out yesterday. Please do it now before it becomes a bigger problem for both of us.'

Arguments are another common trigger. When you discover that you are angry and arguing, withdraw immediately: 'This is not helping. I am getting angry with this. I am going to deal with me, and then I am coming back to deal with you.' This approach lets your children know that you are serious about the situation but that controlling your anger is what you need to do first. Your children will also learn that when you do return, you will be more reasonable and less emotional.

Do not take your child's anger personally, even when he is angry with you. When your child strikes out at you in anger, stay calm. Walk away if needed. This is not easy. If you become angry in return, you are setting up a pattern of power and control, and your child may then seek revenge by becoming angrier.

Chapter 26
How to Talk to Your Children About School Violence

With the upsurge of school violence in America during the past few years, we have become a nation of eyewitnesses. When these tragedies occur, parents and children see the details on television. It is not like watching a film; these images are real and frightening. If your children are old enough to comprehend the situation, you need to be prepared to talk about what they see.

Talk about the facts of the tragedy, but be sensitive to your children's emotional development. Explain only what they need to know to help them understand the situation. Are your children emotionally mature enough to hear the details and not be affected? Do not tell them details that may be too explicit or frightening if it may increase their emotional distress or worry.

Encourage your children to talk about what they have seen and how they feel. Recognize their sadness, fears and concerns. Be honest about your own feelings and fears. Explain that no one knows for sure exactly why these tragedies happen, but it is usually because someone was unhappy and angry. When some people get angry, they become mean and want to hurt others. This is not a good way to think.

Provide comfort and security. Reassure your children that their teachers and head teacher do everything they can to make their schools safe. Talk about things you do to provide safety at home.

Children and Trauma

A trauma or crisis can happen to anyone at any time. School violence is traumatic. So are natural disasters, automobile accidents, suicides, deaths and other sudden emotional losses. These events create tremendous stress and anxiety in children. Emotional reactions vary with each child. Some children become angry and have outbursts, while other children withdraw. Many young children regress into thumb sucking or bed-wetting. Many children have nightmares, lose their appetite, and have trouble sleeping. These reactions may last weeks or months and recur periodically for years.

Parents are the primary source for the safety and security that children require to adjust to these circumstances and emotions. Provide support by talking about your feelings. This will help your children talk about their anger, grief or sadness. Knowing what to say is often difficult. When in doubt, reach out with a firm hug: 'This is sad for both of us.'

If you believe that your child is not adjusting in spite of your best efforts, it may be helpful to talk with other parents or your child's teacher. Most children are affected by tragedies for a few days or a few weeks. If your child's reaction lasts for several weeks or if it recurs periodically, talk to a professional.

Why Have Children Become Violent?

Violence has become entertainment. The American Psychological Association reports that by age eighteen, the average child will have seen 16,000 murders and 200,000 acts of violence in films or on television. In many of these programmes, the images are explicit and graphic, violence is glorified, and the perpetrators are not held accountable or punished. When children are exposed to so many acts of violence, they begin to believe that violence is acceptable. Some children even believe that violence is the preferred way to behave, solve problems, and resolve conflicts. Video games can influence a child to be violent. Many of the 'first-person-shooter' games reward players with points for killing people. Again, children learn that shooting is acceptable and fun.

It would be unfair to say that violence found in the media influences every child the same way. Some children are more resilient, while others are more susceptible. Some children are more influenced by media violence because they have been exposed to real violence in their homes or have themselves been victims.

What You Can Do

Minimize the amount of violence in your children's lives. Preview or review films before your children watch them. If you are unsure about the content of a television programme, watch it with your children. If the programme becomes violent, turn to another station. Many parents have asked my opinion about the 'professional' wrestling programmes on television (not to be confused with the legitimate sport of wrestling). These programmes are very popular, and children want to watch. My opinion is that they have no merit and should not be seen. A good test for any programme that is questionable is that if your child begins to imitate the violence in the programme, he is being influenced and he should not see future programmes.

Know the warning signs. Children who consistently threaten violence often commit violence. Threats may be verbal or non-verbal. Some children draw pictures of violence. All threats need to be considered seriously. Children who exhibit sudden changes in mood or behaviour, such as temper outbursts or increased aggression, may become violent. Children who are fascinated by media violence are more likely to become violent. Children who commit violence against animals are at risk of becoming violent against people. If you experience any of these warning signs with your child, take action. Find a professional to help you help your child. If you have weapons in your home, lock them securely.

Stay connected with your children, especially through adolescence. Do not abdicate your responsibility just because your teenagers say they do not need you any more. Fifteen-year-olds need as much supervision as five-year-olds. Make a date with each of your children at least once a week. Go out for an ice cream and talk. Go for a walk and talk. Your discussions do not have to always include deep thoughts. Even chitchat helps you stay connected.

Teach your children how important it is to be a good friend. When they see a fellow student who appears troubled, reach out to that child. A few words of kindness or even a simple 'hello' can help some children feel better. Many children are unhappy and depressed because they are lonely. By being a good friend and listener, you could prevent someone from becoming angry and violent. Remind your children that when they have a friend who is troubled, it is okay to ask an adult for help.

We live in a world where emotional intelligence is becoming more important than intellectual intelligence. Teach your children to be good decision makers, to manage their own feelings as well as accept and empathize with the feelings of others, and to see diversity as a quality rather than a threat. These skills will give your children a wider scope of vision as well as the self-confidence they need to solve problems without anger, aggression or violence.

Part VI
Simple Solutions to Prevailing Problems

Chapter 27
Resolving Conflicts Between Siblings

Parents often ask about sibling rivalry. Most problems between siblings do not involve rivalry. They involve conflict. Conflicts between children have occurred since Adam and Eve decided that Cain needed a little brother.

Children experience conflicts for many of the same reasons that adults do. Children want the circumstances in their lives to be on their own terms. They want the rules to fit their behaviour rather than fit their behaviour to the rules. Children can only see their side of a situation. Children want everything to go their way. When they do not get what they want, they become angry.

It should not be surprising that any time you put two or three people who think this way into the same confined space and tell them to play and have fun, you are likely to get some conflict. So what can parents do to reduce the amount of conflict amongst their children? Begin by using a conflict as an opportunity to learn. Teach your children acceptable ways of expressing disappointment and resentment. Teach them how to manage their feelings without violating the other person:

> 'You know, Alyssa, it's okay to be angry at your brother for teasing you. But it is not okay to hit him. What else could you have done? Let's think about other things to do when you get angry.'

This approach will not work if your child is still upset about the altercation. Communication is always more effective when everyone has had time to cool off. It also helps to intervene early, before tempers erupt:

> 'It sounds to me like you two may be getting into an argument. I believe that you can work this out for yourselves, and I hope you do. If you need my help, let me know. But if you can't solve this on your own, you will need to take a little break from each other for a while.'

This type of message empowers your children to believe they can resolve their conflict. If you believe they can, they are likely to believe the same. Yet it also sets a limit. Knowing when to become involved and when to keep out takes judgment. As a rule, always encourage your children to solve their own conflicts. Give them time to do this. Then if you see that their conflict is escalating rather than resolving, you may need to guide them to think of a solution. Simply separate them for a few minutes, to give them time to think.

Teach your children to respect the other person, even when they do not agree: 'You do not have to agree with what your brother says. He sees it his way, and you see it your way. It is okay to have different opinions about this, but it's not okay to fight.' This is a skill that will be helpful when they become adults. In some situations, it can also help if you add something about seeing the conflict from the other person's point of view: 'Each of you has a reason for thinking that your opinion is correct.' Then have the children exchange their reasons and develop a compromise. Each child has to give a little so that both can be satisfied.

As a long-term prevention, focus on the positive social behaviours of your children. Compliment your children for getting along. Parents forget this. It is easy to take good behaviour for granted. This is a mistake. Look for co-operation and sharing. Then reinforce it: 'I appreciate you playing together so well. Thank you. I hope you both feel proud of yourselves.'

Perhaps the most important thing a parent can do to teach her children better methods of conflict resolution is to be a good example. Model appropriate ways of solving the conflicts you encounter in your life – with your spouse, your boss, your neighbour, even the irritating salesperson. Do not store anger; express it constructively: 'When you continue to argue, I get angry because it's so frustrating to go around in circles.' Show your children that there are prudent ways to disagree. Model calmness, politeness, and respect for the other person. Remember to be patient. If your children have developed patterns of arguing and fighting, it will take time to change. Hang in there. The children are worth it.

Chapter 28
Responsibility, Chores and Pocket Money

Children need to learn the value of work. When children learn to do work around the house, they are actually learning the basics of independent living skills. Responsibility builds confidence and self-esteem. Work teaches co-operation and teamwork.

Do not give your children too many jobs or responsibilities. This can cause resentment. Accept your child's best effort even though the finished product may not be up to your standard. A good attitude is more important than a perfectly made bed. Being a helper is more important than having all the spoons in the correct drawer divider. Teaching children to work takes more time than doing the work yourself. Use plenty of positive feedback for effort and for jobs well done.

Model appropriate attitudes about work. Children need to see that housework and chores are a part of life. Illustrate the satisfaction you feel when you complete a tough job. Work side by side with your children and have fun. Whistle while you work, so to speak! Let your children have some say in their chores; giving children choices reduces resistance. Assign small responsibilities to young children and then increase the difficulty as they grow older. Responsibilities grow with your child. There are some examples at the end of this chapter.

Model responsibility. Complaining about housework only teaches children to complain. Parents often talk to me about their children's lack of responsibility, yet they are late for appointments. Be prompt. Use 'to-do' lists, check-lists, planners. Teach children these techniques.

As children grow older, they want more privileges. Link responsibilities with privileges: the more you do, the more you earn. Parents expect more from children as they grow. In turn, offer more freedom and more choices. Negotiate responsibilities: 'You think about what is fair, and then we will discuss it.' Some parents have found it helpful to increase privileges and responsibilities with each birthday – a kind of annual promotion.

Talk about goals. Begin early so your children will be familiar with setting goals before they are teenagers. Early goals are experiences such as learning to ride a bicycle, swimming or skating. Goals expand with maturity. What marks do they expect for themselves? What can they achieve athletically? What are reasonable careers? What are the advantages of going to college?

Working for Earnings

Many parents take pocket money away from a child who does not complete all his chores. Make this strategy positive. Use charts as a means to earn pocket money. This works well with any child, and remarkably well with teenagers. Make a list of jobs to do around the house. Call the list 'Moneymakers.' Each job is worth an amount of money. The child who does the job gets the money as part of an pocket money. Distribute jobs fairly among your children. Do not give your child a set pocket money and then take money away. Start each week with no money and let him earn as he works. Children are more able than we think. There are many household jobs children can do. Working teaches children that everyone can pitch in and help.

You can use one chart for all your children's jobs. Assign a start time, a completion time and a point value to each job. Distribute the jobs so that older children work more and earn more. This teaches children that responsibilities and privileges come with age. Rotate jobs when necessary. Each point could be worth five pence.

Moneymaker's Chart

	Mon	Tue	Wed	Thur	Fri
Rachel	Rubbish 7:00—7:10 10 pts		Set table 4:30—4:45 15 pts		Bathroom 4:00—4:30 30 pts
Andy		Set table 4:30—4:45 15 pts		Rubbish 7:00—7:10 10 pts	Furniture 4:00—4:30 30 pts
Jan	Laundry 4:00—4:15 10 pts			Set table 4:30—4:45 15 pts	Vacuum 4:00—4:30 30 pts

This arrangement teaches children to remember when it is time to do a job. If a child fails to start by the appointed time, another child may then do the job and get the points. If Andy has not started to set the table by 4:30, Janelle may set the table. She would then get Andy's 15 points. Andy may want to argue that the job is his. Simply say the job was his until 4:30. At that time it became the job of anyone willing to work.

If the job is not finished by the appointed completion time, your child does not earn the points. Let him finish the job if he chooses, but no points. If he refuses to finish the job, allow another child to finish. Award this child the points.

Be firm but fair. If your child works diligently during the allotted time but does not finish, you have not assigned enough time. In this case, be reasonable. Let the child finish and award him the points. Then change the time on the chart. Start sooner or allow more time to finish. Make this change only if the time turns out to be unfair. Do not change if your child is being stubborn or lazy.

A parent told me that this technique changed her life. Her children stopped arguing about chores. They realized that if they did not work as asked, a brother or sister was going to get their pocket money. If you only have one child, ask a neighbour's child to do the job and then pay him your child's pocket money. You will not have to do this very often.

Teaching Children the Value of Money

Explain the use of money. Begin as early as age three. Explain why and how you buy items at the shop. Money is necessary. Money comes from working: it does not appear by magic from the cash point. My son learned the use of money at age three. He learned that he could play a game of PacMan with one of those 'little round silver things'.

Do not pay for everything. You should not pay your child for everything he does. It is better to assign some jobs as responsibilities without pay. This teaches the idea that we all need to contribute to the success of the family. After your child completes required duties, allow him to pick from a Moneymakers list. Some things you do as part of the family, while some things can earn money. You can also have bonus jobs for earning extra money. When your child or teenager needs some money for a special activity or event, let them earn the money by doing a special job, such as sweeping the garden or polishing the car.

Introduce expenses. As children mature and pocket money increase, require them to use their own money for some things. This applies to dating, films, CDs and other entertainment. Children who want designer labels should pay the additional cost. When Anthony was in the fifth form, he wanted a pair of labelled tennis shoes that retailed for £60. I offered to pay the first £20 – what I would pay for good tennis shoes without the label. The rest of the money was up to him. He went to work in the neighbourhood doing odd jobs. In about a month, he had enough money. He was proud of himself, and wore them every day. He took such good care of these shoes that when he outgrew them a year later, they still looked new. He took such care of them because he had considerable ownership in them.

Teach consumerism. Get children to compare prices. What size package gives the best value? Explain why you choose certain products. Teach about inflation by going to the library and reading ads in old newspapers. This is fun. Remember when a loaf of bread was a quarter of the price? You should know that Anthony did not pay £60 for his shoes. He called all over town until he found them in a sale, for £40. He was a wise consumer, especially with his own money.

Teach home budgeting. Explain how a finite amount of money needs to be distributed for housing, food, clothing, utilities, car expenses, and so on. Do not shelter children from this. Include older children in family financial planning. Let them write out the cheques for the monthly bills.

Start a savings account. Most children comprehend the meaning of savings by the age of ten. Children are impulsive spenders. Encourage your children to save a certain percentage of their income. Some parents match savings.

Start a current account. Most sixteen-year-olds are ready for a limited current account and limited credit card. Teach them to manage these tools while you are still around to keep things from getting out of control.

Set financial goals. Discuss plans for paying for college. Research college scholarships and other assisted places. Get them to calculate tuition costs and living expenses.

Let them earn their own money. The best way for children to learn about money is for them to get their own job when they are legally old enough. Help them find a job that is safe, has reasonable hours and includes friendly people. Having your own income is a great self-esteem booster.

Do not overdo it! Children need to learn about the value of money. They need to learn how to earn and manage money. But do not worship money. Spending money on something impractical occasionally is fun and human.

Chores and Pocket Money

Many parents give children a weekly allowance, then take money away for not completing work. Reverse this — use a positive strategy.

- Start each week with no money and build up. (work = pocket money).
- Specific jobs earn a certain amount of money.
- Be sure jobs are age appropriate.
- Do not pay children for everything they do around the house.
- Some jobs are required, some are for pocket money.
- Required jobs must be done first.
- Have bonus jobs available for extra money when needed.

How to Teach Your Children About Responsibility

Sit down with each of your children and divide activities and responsibilities into three categories. Some things are required behaviours; some things are negotiated; some things are totally up to your child. Make a list for each category. As your child grows and shows responsibility, move more items toward the bottom list. For example, wearing make-up may start on the negotiated list. Give your daughter some choice about her use of make-up, but you still have to approve. As she matures and shows good taste in her use of make-up, you could move this activity to the bottom list: 'You have shown that you use make-up correctly. From now on, you won't need to check with me. I trust you to take care of this yourself.' This strategy will help your child see the value in responsible behaviour.

Requirements **What your child has to do.**

> Pass exams
>
> Help with work around the house

Negotiated **Your child has some choice but needs your approval.**

> Agreed time to be home
>
> TV programmes
>
> Make-up
>
> Snacks

Self-Control **Your child has total responsibility.**

> Sports
>
> Music
>
> School activities

Age-Appropriate Responsibilities

3- to 4-year-olds

Brush teeth

Put dirty clothes in the laundry basket

Match socks

Put clean clothes away with assistance

Help tidy up room and toys

4- to 5-year-olds

Help set or clear table of unbreakables

Water plants

Feed pets

Get the mail or newspaper, with parent watching

Wash and dry plastic dishes

Help load dishwasher with safe items

6- to 8-year-olds

Clean own room

Take care of most personal hygiene

Help fold and sort laundry

Make beds

Put away groceries

Set and clear table

Wash and dry dishes (other than sharp objects)

Take out rubbish

Sweep floors

9- to 12-years-olds

All personal hygiene

Polish furniture

Prepare parts of meals
Do some laundry
Help in the garden
Vacuum carpet
Mop floors
Prepare own snacks
Help with grocery shopping
Purchase clothing with assistance
Clean the garage
Wash the car

13- to 15-year-olds

Baby-sit
Mow lawns
Clean windows
Help with heavy cleaning
Do own laundry
Do some ironing
Budget own money
Shop for own clothing
Do neighbourhood jobs
Do small repairs
Prepare some meals

16 years plus

Do outside jobs for money
Plan and prepare meals
Travel with supervision
Take care of all clothing needs
Help care for the car
Plan higher education goals

Chapter 29
Homework Hassles

Homework is one of the greatest sources of conflict between children and parents. Children avoid doing homework. They procrastinate until the last minute, fail to bring work home, make excuses, do as little as possible, take too long or do it too fast, and do not do their best. Parents become frustrated and angry with these attitudes and behaviours. The source of this frustration is often disappointment: we want perfect apples. Parents become embarrassed when children perform poorly on their homework – what will the teacher think of them?

Most parents realize the value of homework, but most children do not. Parents know that homework reinforces skills; practise makes perfect. Children see homework as repetitive and boring. Parents know that children who do quality homework learn more and get better marks, while some children see homework as a penalty for not getting everything done at school.

Parents and teachers need to be partners in the development of healthy homework habits. Teachers need to explain the value of homework to their students; that homework is to help you learn, that it affects your grades and your future, develops responsibility, independence, accountability and personal organization skills, and that it teaches children to manage their time.

Teachers have a responsibility to ensure that homework is not boring, as well as that it is well within the child's ability level. The assignment must be fair. If your child works for a solid hour to do an assignment that looks as if it should take ten minutes, speak to the teacher immediately. The homework needs to be modified. This is assuming that your child is working diligently, not dawdling.

Teachers should also have an incentive programme that motivates children to complete homework on time and with their best effort. Some teachers use class charts: students who successfully complete homework earn stars that are traded for class activity time. Most primary teachers agree with using an incentive programme, but some secondary school teachers do not agree with using incentives. These teachers believe that children should do homework because it is a demonstration of responsibility. This is true; children need to learn the value of studying. However, if a child does not have the internal motivation to complete homework, charts and contracts often provide some external motivation to get things going in the right direction. If your child is not motivated and the teacher does not have an incentive programme, you can develop a programme at home.

How to Be a Homework Facilitator

There are several factors to consider when developing successful homework strategies. Visit or call your child's teacher and ask about his or her homework policy. How often will homework be given? How much homework will there be? What subjects? Ask to be notified in advance when special projects are set. When are the tests? Will there be study guides? This information will enable you to develop a better homework plan.

Children need to know that doing homework is their job, not yours. Many parents have to stand over their children each night. Every assignment is a struggle. Homework is between your child and his teacher. You are only a facilitator. Your job is to help, not to do it for him. Do not make this mistake. If you are already trapped in this dilemma, stop tonight. Tell your child that your responsibility is to help – his responsibility is to complete the homework. Here is what you can do to help.

Be sure your child has enough time to do homework. Children are involved in many activities: athletics, music lessons, dance class, scouts, church clubs. These are excellent, but homework must be the priority. Have a set time for homework each day. Negotiate this time with your children if possible. Reschedule around other activities only when necessary. Check with your child's teacher to determine how much time will be needed. If your child has no homework, he can read from his favourite book for thirty minutes. The same is true for a child who 'forgets' his homework. These techniques let children know that homework is important.

Have a specific place to do homework. This place should be distraction free. Turn off the TV during homework time. Parents can set an example by reading. Be sure your child has a table and chair. The kitchen table works fine, as long as there is quiet. Be sure there is adequate lighting. Have all necessary supplies nearby so that homework time is not spent hunting for glue or tape or paper. Your child's teacher can give you a list of items to put into a supply box. Older children may need a calculator and eventually a computer.

Some children resist doing homework. First, be sure the child can do the homework. Check with the teacher. If ability is not the problem, it may be that your child sees the assignment(s) as overwhelming. If so, breaking the assignment into more manageable parts will promote success. Preview the assignment with your child; read the directions and check for understanding. Do the first question or problem with your child. This will let him know that it is not so difficult. Provide encouragement at each step: 'You do the next three on your own. Then I'll come back and check them.' Tell your child that you have confidence in his ability to complete the work and do his best: 'You did the first one correctly, I bet you can do the next three and get them all right.' Be available to answer questions.

Some children resist doing homework because they question the relevance of the assignment: 'Why do I have to do that? It's stupid.' 'I did this last year, I am not doing it again.' Unfortunately, not every assignment has equal meaning to every child. Some assignments may be irrelevant and boring. These assignments must be done anyway. You do not have to like it, but you have to do it. This is how the real world operates. We all have aspects of our jobs that are irrelevant and boring. We get used to it.

Teach children to do the worst first. If your child has difficulty with maths, do it first, get it over and feel relieved. The remaining assignments will be less threatening. Doing the worst first makes more sense because your child is more alert mentally.

Some children speed through their assignments. This is only a problem if the work is sloppy or inaccurate. If the work is neat and correct, homework is finished for the day. Do not penalize your child for working quickly, as long as he is accurate. If the work is sloppy or inaccurate, tell your child redo the assignment. If you anticipate that your child may be a speeder, let him know your rules ahead of time.

Homework Incentives

For most children, the organization and planning strategies discussed above, along with some verbal encouragement, are enough to get successful homework habits started, but for some children these tactics are not enough. Some children are reluctant. Some children dawdle. These children need stronger incentives.

Use computers and educational software to motivate your children. Hundreds of software programmes reinforce reading, spelling and maths skills. Interactive encyclopaedias and history and science programmes on CD-ROM and on-line research services are fun and exciting learning tools.

Check-lists, charts and contracts are good motivators. Have daily, weekly or long-term payoffs. Make a list of the specific activities that your child must follow in order to improve homework habits.

The check-list below emphasizes the importance of taking responsibility. Children must realize that school success and doing homework is for them, not you. You already have your education. They should do well in school to please themselves.

Punishment does not motivate children to do better in school, or to do their best on homework. You cannot make your child learn; motivation to learn and do schoolwork can only be achieved through encouragement and self-discipline. Avoid homework power struggles. Arguments over homework only provide your children with another button to push.

	Mon	Tue	Wed	Thur	Fri
Write down assignments					
Bring materials home					
Start on time					
Work independently					
Be neat and accurate					
Check your work					
Finish on time					
Hand it in					

Chapter 30
Attention Deficits, Hyperactivity and Behaviour

All children can be divided into two groups: hard to raise and harder to raise. Parents often ask why it happens that all of their children are well behaved except one, who gives them all the grief. I experienced this phenomenon with a teenager early in my career. The youngster was fourteen. His father was a very prominent and successful secondary school principal and his mother was a teacher. There were nine children in this family: eight were very successful in all aspects of life, but this one was a delinquent. I am not sure that anyone can fully explain this.

Why Is This Child So Difficult?

I have listened to hundreds of parents tell me that their child has been 'difficult since birth'. Children have different temperaments, skills, interests and abilities. Children also behave differently. Knowing why one child is more difficult than the others is not important; knowing how to handle the situation is. Difficult children require more of your time and energy. If you want all of your children to be successful, and you have one or two children who are particularly hard to raise, it simply means that you will have to be more actively engaged in parenting.

Children with attention deficit disorder (ADD) present a special challenge to parents and teachers. Children with ADD have a poor attention span and are more impulsive than the average child of the same age. Many ADD children are also hyperactive. These children have attention deficit hyperactivity disorder (ADHD). Treatment for a true ADD/ADHD child typically includes four aspects: medical management, often with medication; educational planning; individual and family counselling; and behaviour planning. Here is an example of a behaviour plan that can be used with an ADD/ADHD child, or any child with special needs.

Planning for Difficult Children

Some children have attention deficits and hyperactivity that cause impulsive behaviour. Misbehaviour may increase due to your child's frustration. Some children who have allergies take medications that affect their moods and may agitate their activity levels, factors that make discipline more difficult. You will need to use careful judgement in deciding what is a misbehaviour and what is the effect of the disorder. Be extra positive and consistent during these periods.

Tommy is more active than usual today. He is all over the

place. Mum is not sure what to do. She has seen bad days before. She used to make excuses and let Tommy do as he pleased on days like this, but she has learned that excuses did not help Tommy learn to control his problem. Now she has a plan. As soon as Mum notices that Tommy is getting too excited or energetic, she takes him aside: 'Tommy, you are letting yourself get too active. You need to settle down. You are having a good day so far, I do not want to see you get into trouble. Let me sit with you for a few minutes. I'll read you a story. You take a couple of deep breaths and relax.'

Here is Mum's plan. (This plan works well for any child.) She knows that it is important to intervene early. She steps in as soon as she notices Tommy getting active. If she waited until he was out of control, it would be much more difficult to settle him down. Mum has also learned to stay calm. Her calmness influences Tommy to be calm. If she becomes angry or yells, Tommy will get worse. Mum stays with Tommy. She does not just tell him to 'settle down' and leave it up to him to settle down by himself. Mum gets Tommy involved with a quiet activity, such as listening to a story. She asks him to take a few deep breaths to help him relax. This will redirect Tommy. Some children can be redirected by soft music, listening to headphones, listening to a story on cassette tape, or watching television.

After a while, Tommy may only need a cue. A cue is a special signal from a parent that reminds a child to get control. If Mum and Tommy practise this technique consistently each time he gets too excited, they will build a pattern. Tommy will learn to give himself feedback about his activity level. Eventually, he will learn to control himself. I worked with a parent whose cue to her son was, 'You need to go to the beach.' Her son liked relaxing at the ocean. When he got his signal, he would spread a towel on his bed and lie down and think about being by the sea.

Remedies at Home

Children like Tommy require consistency. They need structure and routine. Set up schedules for waking up, mealtimes, job times, homework, TV, play time, etc. Use a clock or a timer to increase understanding and motivation. Do not change this routine unless you let your child know in advance.

Have specific rules written down. It may be helpful to use a chart or contract. Also have specific consequences written down in advance, punishments as well as incentives.

Use clear language when giving instructions, and demonstrate when you can. Keep it simple. Do not give more than one or two instructions at a time. Ask your child to repeat the instructions to you before he begins to do something.

Provide your child with a quiet place to settle down. You can use this place to read or do homework. Keep this place distraction free.

Stay calm. Children like Tommy can be frustrating, but getting angry usually aggravates the situation.

Many children who are like Tommy need consistent follow-through when they do not behave. Time-out has proved to be an excellent way of teaching children with special problems.

Of course, the ideas in this chapter will work with any child as well as children with special problems. Do not use disabilities as excuses for misbehaviour. You will be teaching your child that his weakness is a crutch to use as an excuse the rest of his life. Tommy has an attention deficit disorder. He says, 'I can't behave today because I forgot my pill,' because his parents have taught him that his pill controls his behaviour. Children with disabilities need to be taught that the only way to overcome their weakness is by diligence and hard work. Excuses only handicap them more. Children with special problems need special plans, not excuses. Focus your time, energy and consistency on the difficult children, and the not-so-difficult children will get through life with your love and discipline.

Chapter 31
Divorce

Lisa was the kind of student teachers would call on when they wanted an imaginative answer. She had a reputation for having a cheery and sociable disposition, and was blessed with intelligence, personality and self-confidence. She earned good marks and was a leader among her peers. The world was an exciting place for Lisa. She was optimistic and enthusiastic about her life and her future.

Then her life changed – suddenly and almost completely. She went from first-class student to school failure, from cheerful to withdrawn, from leader to loser. She became unsure of herself, inattentive, forgetful and depressed. School was simply not that important to her any more.

What caused this dreadful transformation? Lisa was suffering from an affliction that has no name but strikes as many as 80 per cent of the children in some schools. Lisa's parents got a divorce.

How Children Think

When I first met Lisa, she did everything she could to convince me that she was not having any problems. Lisa's reaction is typical. Like most children who experience the distress of divorce, she could not explain why she was doing poorly in school, and she did not want anyone to know she was hurting inside. She did not want to say anything that might intensify the difficulties at home. Children see the stress their parents are going through; they fear that exposing their emotions will only add to everyone's misery. This is why most children never talk to their parents about their feelings concerning the divorce. These hidden feelings increase anxiety and weaken a child's ability to perform in school. Additionally, repressed feelings may become the seeds for larger problems later in life.

Finally, Lisa talked about her feelings:

> 'What do you think about your parents getting divorced?'
> 'I don't like it.'
> 'What do you mean?'
> 'My Mum cries a lot.'
> 'How does that make you feel?'
> 'Sad. I wish she would stop.'
> 'Do you know why your parents got divorced?'
> 'They used to fight a lot.'
> 'Did they ever fight about you?'
> 'Yes.'
> 'Do you feel it was your fault that your parents got divorced?'
> 'Yes. It was all my fault.'

With these words, tears filled Lisa's eyes. I handed her a box of tissues and told her that it was okay to cry. She wept openly for several minutes. She was dumping some of the emotional rubbish she had been carrying for months. When she caught her breath, she explained.

'Once was standing in front of the TV, and my Dad yelled at me to move. Then my Mum yelled at him to stop yelling at me. Then they got in a big fight, and my Dad left the house. Two weeks later they told me they were getting a divorce. So I think they are getting a divorce because of me.'

Lisa was overcome by guilt. She was feeling responsible for her parents' divorce. Over half of the children I speak to feel that they were the primary reason for the divorce. They think, 'If only I had been better behaved or done a better job on my chores. If only I had kept my room clean or received better marks, my parents would still be together. If I had been a better child, none of this would have happened.' This self-blame can create overwhelming feelings of poor self-worth, insecurity and depression. When a child feels guilty or depressed, school is simply not that important.

What Happens in School

Twenty-five years ago, the divorce rate was not high enough to merit much attention. It's different today, and we have learned a lot along the way. Divorce hurts children, and hurt children strike back, sometimes at themselves. Loss, rejection, abandonment, loneliness, fear, guilt, stress and anger hit hard. Most observers see a connection between the divorce rate and increased rates of gang delinquency, drug use and dropouts.

Because many of the schoolchildren referred to me for learning or behaviour problems have experienced a divorce, I have learned a lot about the ways that divorce affects children in school. I have also learned some things about prevention and treatment.

Children psychologically bond to both parents. When parents divorce, it is like having half of your personality torn away. When children feel like half of their 'self' is missing, feelings of loss, rejection and abandonment destroy their ability to concentrate in school.

These unhealthy feelings increase when parents attack or degrade each other. When one parent says malicious things about the other in front of the children, the children worry that these displeasing qualities exist in them. 'If Dad is a bad person, am I a bad person too? After all, I'm a lot like my dad.'

When parents try to get even or outdo each other, the children become confused. I worked with one family where the mother insisted that the children be sheltered from violence, a reasonable request. Dad's favourite weekend activities: Stallone movies on the video and afternoon trips to the rifle range. While the parents argued about what was best for the children, the children became divided and emotionally unsteady.

Some children of divorce lose contact with one of their parents. Nathan's parents have been divorced for five years. His father has remarried and has children with his new wife. Over the years, Nathan has gradually lost his relationship with his father:

'I feel like no one likes me.'
'Do you feel that way because your dad doesn't
   see you?'
'Yes.'
'What do you mean?'
'It must be me. He doesn't like me for some reason.'
'Do you think you have done something wrong?'
'I must have done something. Maybe I'm a bad kid.'
'Do you think you are a bad kid?'
'Yes.'
'How often do you feel that way?'
'All the time.'
'How often do you think about your father?'
'Every day.'

Nathan's feelings of rejection and loss cut deep. He believes that he is a worthless child. He is sure that his lack of paternal contact means that he is not worthy of his father's love and time. He thinks about it every day, and his lack of self-worth interferes with every aspect of his life. He is afraid to make friends, to do well in school, or even to get too close to his mother. If his father did not care, if his father left him, others would too.

Some children worry about being abandoned by the caretaking parent. If one parent has left me, how do I know my other parent won't leave me? Who will take care of me? This is another reason why children do not talk to their parents about their feelings. A seven-year-old once explained, 'My mum is very angry with my dad. If I tell her how sad I am, she will get madder. Then she might leave me, too.' Children are afraid to say or do anything that will alienate or provoke their parents for fear that both may leave.

Anger and aggression are typical reactions to divorce. This is especially true when the parents get angry with each other. Steven's parents had been divorced for several months. During that time, Steven had been getting more aggressive at school and at home. What caused the increased anger and aggression? Steven was angry at his dad – for leaving, for not spending more time with him, for having a new girlfriend. Steven did not direct his anger at Dad; that might drive Dad away even more. Steven took it out on peers, because it was relatively safe to do so. He also took his anger out on his little sister, because she liked Dad's new girlfriend.

Steven was also angry at his father because there was not as much money as there once was: 'I'm mad because we are poor now. We can't do things like we used to. My dad has all the money.' Children soon learn that divorce lowers financial status, and they worry about basic needs and routine. How will we buy food? Will we have to move into a cheaper home? When will I ever get some new clothes? What about the new bike I was supposed to get? Can I still be in the football team? It is difficult to think about the French Revolution when you don't know how the bills are going to be paid.

Change frightens children. Often, one parent takes the children and leaves home. They may move in with relatives or into less expensive quarters. For many children, this means a new home, new school, new friends and new stresses. Add this to the loss of a parent and a radical change in lifestyle, and you have the ingredients for an emotional trauma. These changes interfere with success at school.

Some children fear being stolen by an angry or vengeful parent. This fear develops when parents make threats or hostile remarks, like, 'I'll take the kids away from you, and you'll never see them again.' This often occurs when one parent is denied access to the children. As a result, children are afraid to walk to school, walk home, or be in a predicament where they might be kidnapped.

Over half of the children I speak to hope their parents will get back together. It is understandable for children to think in this manner. Children want the family to be the way it used to be. This is a fantasy that most children grasp at regardless of the facts. A first-year university student once told me that he frequently thinks about reuniting his parents. They have been divorced since he was six, and both parents have been remarried for years, but he still hangs on to the possibility.

Delayed Effects

The aftermath of divorce lasts for years. A mother came to speak to me about her seventeen-year-old daughter. Melody had always done well at school. She was a well-behaved and trustworthy young lady. Within a two-month period it all turned around; Melody quit going to school, became promiscuous and got involved with drugs. When I spoke with Melody, she knew exactly what was going on inside herself. She was angry at her father, who had left her and her mother when Melody was seven, and she kept hoping he would return. If he did, she wanted to be sure he would be proud of her, so she always did well for him. Then recently, she realized he was never coming back. 'So why be good?' she said. 'I decided to stop working so hard and have a good time instead.'

It had been ten years since Melody's father left. It took ten years for the hurt and loss to fester to the point where it finally erupted, and for the effects to become visible. It would be easy to dismiss a ten-year-old event as probable cause for a recent change in behaviour. I now realize that the impact of divorce may be immediate, but it may not surface for years. Teachers and other school professionals must be aware of this when working with troubled children. Do not overlook a divorce as influencing a child's behaviour or mood just because it happened several years ago. It may still be fresh in the child's mind.

Monday Morning Re-entry

The most common debilitating effect of divorce is Monday morning re-entry after a weekend with Dad (or Mum). Many children of divorce see their non-custodial parent only on weekends, usually two weekends a month. Upon returning from the weekend visit, many children go through a period of adjustment that may last for several days. Some children withdraw, daydream, and show a lack of motivation. Other children act up, becoming short-tempered, belligerent and oppositional. Some children become vengeful and aggressive.

Several years ago, when divorce was less common, teachers and parents assumed that the Monday morning re-entry behaviour was caused by a weekend of freedom with no limits and no discipline. The popular conclusion was that the children should see less of this parent. It is true that weekend parents have a tendency to indulge their children; but Monday morning re-entry is the result of something else.

We now realize that this phenomenon is probably caused by seeing too little of the weekend parent, for at least two reasons. First, a weekend is barely enough time to get acquainted with someone on an intimate or affectionate level. Just as the parent and children start warming to each other, it's over. The children relive the loss of a parent every other Sunday night. Since it takes several days to deal with this loss, the re-entry behaviour results.

Second, many weekend parents feel like outsiders in their children's lives. The parent and children do not see enough of each other to learn each other's likes, dislikes, interests, emotions, or patterns of behaviour. Weekend parents do not get to know their children, and weekend children do not get to know their parent. The result: the Disneyland syndrome. Weekend parents have a tendency to pack the weekend with expensive, fun-filled activities, gifts and junk food. This does two things. It tells the children that this parent is nice. It also eliminates any need for routine discipline. Children do not misbehave when they are being stuffed with goodies and entertainment.

What's the cure? More time with the weekend parent. Increased contact eliminates the feelings of loss, and the re-entry behaviours are diminished. More time with the weekend parent also neutralizes the Disneyland effects. As this parent becomes more involved with the children, more routine time will occur. This parent will develop a wider view of the children's lives and will become more committed to all aspects of the children, including discipline. This usually leads to more co-operation and consistency between the parents. The result is a more stable environment for the children. The children end up doing better for both parents and better in school as well.

A Child's Three Wishes

The effects of divorce on children cannot be eliminated, but their impact can be reduced. What follows is a list of optimal circumstances that may not always be easy for parents to accomplish, but are always best for children.

Wish 1. *Children should have free access to both parents. They should be able to phone or see either parent without fear of offending the other parent. Children should not have to choose between parents. This creates a lose-lose situation. Children need permission to love both parents in front of each parent.*

What about the circumstance where one parent is far away? Many absent parents mistakenly believe that the children they left behind are better off without them. Not true. Encourage as much contact as possible. Write letters and make phone calls. Children love E-mail. Send messages on cassette tapes or videos. Send pictures. Post copies of school reports and invitations to events. Visit on bank holidays and during the summer holidays. If a parent refuses contact, explain that it is not the child's fault; lack of contact does not make the child a worthless person. Provide frequent reassurance by pointing out the lovable qualities in the child.

There are some situations where contact should be restricted. For example, a parent who has abused the children should have supervised visits. In situations such as this, the children should receive counselling.

Wish 2. *Children want consistency to feel safe and secure. Parents need to establish similar rules and consequences at both homes. Parents need periodically to discuss and agree on daily routine, such as allowable foods and snacks, films, bedtime, bathtime, homework, church, and so on. A co-operative spirit tells children that both parents are likable people. Children want pleasant parents as much as parents want pleasant children. Consistency gives children balance and helps them adjust to the divorce situation. Better adjustment means better performance at school.*

Many single parents feel guilty. Guilty parents have a tendency to give in to misbehaviour. They make excuses: 'It's not his fault. He is confused right now.' Giving in to misbehaviour is a mistake. Be consistent. Be understanding and supportive, but do not let children misbehave. Children need limits and consistency.

Wish 3. *Children should know that both parents are still involved in their lives. Parents do not divorce their children. Children need dual parenting. This goes beyond joint custody. Children need both parents actively participating in all aspects of their lives, particularly school. Both parents should attend parent/teacher meetings, if not together, then separately. Both parents should attend school functions. They can sit apart or take turns going to events. Dual involvement clearly indicates that both parents believe that school is a priority. This makes doing well at school more important to the child.*

What Schools Can Do

Schools have a responsibility to stay in touch with both parents, even if the custodial parent does not like it. Schools should provide a model for best practice. Since children do better when both parents are involved in the education process, schools need to make every effort to include both parents – send two school reports, set up two teacher/parent meetings, send two invitations to school events, and call both parents when the child has a good day. This will create a more stable and supportive home-school-home environment.

Teachers should also be aware that children of divorce often exhibit emotional and behavioural problems. They should provide support and encouragement during difficult times. They must be good listeners and allow time for the child to talk about his feelings. A teacher may be the only adult with whom the child is willing to talk.

Blended and Extended Families

Remarriage often creates blended families. A blended family includes children who are his, hers and theirs. Several children from different marriages may live together at different times of the week or month or year. It's confusing. That is why it is even more important that parents be consistent in these situations. More consistency means less confusion.

Consistency is important in extended families. I worked with a family where a six-year-old lived with her mother, her uncle, and her two grandparents. She had four parents. Everyone was giving her different messages. The uncle was Mr. Nice Guy. Anything she did was permissible to him. The grandparents were always trying to get her to behave by bribing her with goodies. Mum had to be the heavy. She did all the punishing and yelling and screaming and threatening. When the mother came to me for counselling, I listened during our first session.

For our second meeting, we had a group session with Mum, Uncle, Grandma and Grandpa. We spent the entire session talking about consistency; rules, bedtime, snacks, and so on.

There are many forms of families today. All of them can produce normal, well-behaved and self-disciplined children. Children adjust to most family situations, but their adjustment is faster and healthier when parents – whoever they are – are consistent.

Millions of children have been hurt by divorce. Until recently, we assumed that the natural flexibility and resiliency built into all children would guarantee their survival. We now know differently. Children must feel good about themselves in order to behave and to perform well at school. Emotional conflict, anxiety, stress and fear interrupt the natural growth process.

Children adjust to divorce better and therefore do better in school when both parents are part of their lives. There is no cure for divorce, but there is treatment. Keep peace between the parents and keep both parents in the children's lives. The greater the harmony between parents, the better the adjustment for the children. It's that simple.

I realize that many parents who have been through a hostile divorce are thinking that these suggestions are unrealistic. That may be so, but I am writing about what is best for children. What is best for children is consistency between parents.

Chapter 32
Peer Pressure

Billy came home from school with tears in his eyes. He was the only student in his class who got 100 per cent in the maths test. All his friends teased him, calling him a 'swot'. If you want to be popular at school, it's better to be good at football than be good at maths.

How Peer Pressure Works

Peer pressure is the influence that children have on each other. Peers can have a positive influence, and sometimes they do. Unfortunately, some peer pressure is negative. There is pressure to join gangs, to drink and do drugs, to have sex, to do poorly in school.

Children are susceptible to peer pressure from the time they start school. Peer pressure occurs in the classroom, in the playground, in the dining room, or anywhere children gather. Withstanding negative peer pressure is a problem for children and teenagers. The message is: Be a part of the crowd. Don't stand out. Don't be unique. Be like everyone else. Don't have the best clothes. Don't have the worst clothes. Don't get the highest marks. Don't get the lowest marks. Be somewhere in the middle.

Most teenagers are their own worst critics. They catastrophize their shortcomings. That's why they spend so much time in front of mirrors. They need to look perfect on the outside because they are confused on the inside. Our society promotes looking perfect. The average child sees 350,000 commercials by the age of sixteen, with messages like 'Buy our cereal and be more athletic,' or 'Use our toothpaste, and your love will last forever.'

From the time they are young, teach your children that happiness comes from the inside, never the outside. Every individual is different. Everyone has strengths and weaknesses, pros and cons, good points and bad points. It's normal to be different. Teach your children to focus on what they do well. Do not dwell on imperfections. Say, for instance,

> 'Not everyone can be great at football. Some people are more athletic than others. You have other strong points. You are very kind. Everyone who knows you likes you. You have a pleasant sense of humour. Your marks are always good. Don't put yourself down about football. Do your best and enjoy the game.'

Your child's best defence against peer pressure is confidence. Arm your child with self-worth by pointing out strengths and successes. Teach him to have integrity: 'You have always been able to stand up for yourself and do what you know is right. You should be proud of yourself for that.' This will teach your child to believe in himself and his ability to make choices. Talk to your children about self esteem. Tell them it's all right to feel low about yourself. Teach them to talk to someone when they feel sad or depressed. Let them know they can come to you with any problem.

> 'It's okay to be down occasionally. It happens to everyone. When I feel low, talking seems to help. If I

talk about what's bothering me, the problem doesn't feel so big. Mum and I talk about problems to each other all the time. It helps us feel better. You decide what you want to do. No matter what it is, I'll be here if you need me.'

Encourage your children to talk to other children about feelings: 'I know you have a good friend you can talk to about this. I bet she has the same fears and worries about the dance that you have. Talk with her. You may both feel better.'

Remind your children that no one has all the answers. It's normal to feel unsure of yourself at times. When children see that other children feel the way they do, they realize it's common. They don't feel so alone and scared, or so hopeless.

Let your house be a place for teenagers to hang out. Give them some privacy. Let them listen to music, talk and play games. Whenever you can, compliment the group about their friendship: 'I'm glad to see you get along so well. Having good friends makes growing up a little easier.' Teach your teenagers to support each other. Be friends with people who like you for what you are. Teach your children to stay away from peers who are critical: 'Not everyone has the same sense of right and wrong. Stay away from kids who put you down and make you feel bad. Let them be the way they are without you. If you can influence them to do better, great – but do not let them influence you to do less.'

There may be peer pressures at school that you cannot change. Involve your children with other groups. Get them involved with church groups, scouts, or other groups that are supportive.

Listening Builds Trust

Troubled teenagers say, 'I can't talk to my parents. They don't understand me. They don't know anything about me. I don't trust them. They don't trust me.'

Successful teenagers say, 'I know I can tell my parents anything. They listen to my problems. I'm not afraid to tell them when something has gone wrong. They trust me.' Successful children have parents who are good listeners.

When children and teenagers have problems, they need to know they can come to you for help. When they do not feel safe coming to you for help, they often face their problems alone. For some children and teenagers, this is all right. For others, it is not. Many children who cannot face their problems alone try to escape their problems. Common escapes are gangs, drinking, drugs and suicide.

Respect promotes healthy listening. We often show more courtesy to strangers than to our children. Are you as polite to your children as you are to your boss or your neighbour? Show respect for your children and they will learn to respect you and themselves. When you speak to your children, show trust, confidence and acceptance, and they will do the same:

> 'I would like to hear what you think.'
> 'I trust your ideas on . . .'
> 'I may not agree with you, but it's good to say what you feel.'
> 'I may not have listened well the last time we talked. I'm sorry. If you will give me another chance, I would like to listen to you now.'

Be attentive when your children speak to you. It is easy to be distracted by your surroundings – the television, telephone interruptions, or other children making noise. Anger can be a distraction. It is difficult to pay attention and think clearly when you are upset. It is easy to become preoccupied with your own thoughts – worries about money, mentally reviewing items at work, or getting dinner ready.

There were many times when my children wanted to talk to me while I was engrossed in writing this book. It was not always easy to turn away and listen. There were times when I would ask them to wait: 'I'm in the middle of an important idea. Can you come back in three minutes?' It is better to be honest than to pretend to listen.

Take care of your distractions and preoccupations and then focus on your child. Look at him. Let him know that you believe talking is important. It may be helpful to find a quiet place where you will be free from interruptions and distractions. Go for a ride or a walk. Go and sit in the park. This will emphasize the importance of the communication for both of you. This lets him know that what he says is important. It tells him he can talk to you about anything. This takes practice and commitment. Be open to anything he says. No matter how bizarre or frightening, listen without blame or judgement. If he says something that makes your stomach flip, try clarifying.

How to Clarify and Express Feelings

Clarifying means rephrasing your child's statement. Listen for the hidden feeling or meaning in what your child says. When you think you have it figured out, use clarifying to check your perception. Here is how many parents react:

LISA: 'Trisha is a jerk.'
MUM: 'Don't talk that way. I've told you that before.'

The tone of Mum's response is critical. Mum is responding to Lisa's words. Mum's response is closed. It shuts down further communication. Lisa will not say much more about her problem or her feelings.

LISA: 'Trisha is a jerk.'
MUM: 'Are you angry at Trisha?'
LISA: 'Yes. She told the other girls I like Brian.'

In this example, Mum's response is open-ended, so Lisa keeps on talking. Mum perceives that Lisa is angry. She checks it out. This lets Lisa know that Mum is listening. Your first perception may not always be correct. Open responses will encourage children to keep talking anyway. Incorrect open responses are better than closed responses.

LISA:	'Trisha is a jerk.'
MUM:	'Are you angry at Trisha?'
LISA:	'I'm not angry. I'm hurt. She didn't invite me to her party.'

Being a good listener means hearing beyond the words. Use clarifying to keep your child talking about his feelings and the problem. Do not respond with criticism, judgement or advice. Keep your opinion to yourself until your child wants to listen. Then use guiding questions to teach your child to think for himself.

Teaching Children to Think for Themselves

Parents enjoy giving their children advice. We like to solve their problems for them. We like to protect them from making a wrong decision. We like to give them the answers. We do not like waiting for them to generate their own alternatives. In most situations, this is harmless. Sometimes it's not. There are times when they need to think for themselves. Your goal is to teach your child to think before acting. Teenagers need to think for themselves when they face peer pressure, decisions about drugs and sex, and school problems.

Children need to practise solving their problems when they are young, so they will know how when they are teenagers. Rather than provide solutions, teach your children how to generate their own alternatives.

The following questioning technique will allow you to guide your child's thinking while he makes a decision.

'What did you do?'
'What were you supposed to do? (or, 'What is the rule?')

'Did you make the right choice?' (or, 'Was that a
   good decision?')
'What could you have done differently?'
'What could you do next time?'

These questions are suggestions. You may develop your
own technique that works as well. Here is a dialogue between
Mum and twelve-year-old Kayla. This is an example of how to
use guiding questions.

MUM: 'What did you do, Kayla?'
KAYLA: 'She was baiting me.'
MUM: 'Just tell me what you did.'
KAYLA: 'I hit her.'
MUM: 'What's the rule about hitting?'
KAYLA: 'But she was calling me names, too.'
MUM: 'Did you hit?'
KAYLA: 'Yes.'
MUM: 'Was that a good decision?'
KAYLA: (Silence.)
MUM: 'What else could you have done besides
           hitting?'
KAYLA: 'I could have walked away.'
MUM: 'That's right. That might have been a better
           choice. Would you be in trouble if you had
           walked away?'
KAYLA: 'No.'
MUM: 'Maybe you should try that the next time
           someone baits you.'

Mother would not accept excuses and would not let Kayla
distract her. She was teaching Kayla to think about what she did
and develop alternatives for the future.

When your child cannot think of alternatives, refrain from
giving advice. If you give advice and it does not work, it's your
fault. Give suggestions by telling a story: 'When I was your age,
I had a friend who had a similar situation. She solved her problem by ignoring the kids who were teasing her.' This strategy

plants the idea. Leave it up to your child to make the choice. (I do not feel this is deceit. I am sure this happened to one of my friends at some point.)

By asking the right questions, you can avoid arguments and teach your child how to make better decisions. Here is an example of a case that is more difficult.

DAD: 'What happened, Kevin?'

KEVIN: 'Nothing happened.'

DAD: 'What did you do?'

KEVIN: 'I said nothing happened.'

DAD: 'It looks to me like you hit your brother.'

KEVIN: 'Then why did you ask if you already know?'

DAD: 'We have spoken about this before. You know that hitting is not permitted in this house. I hope that the next time this occurs, you make a better decision. We can decide what to do about this later.'

Dad makes the point about decision making in spite of Kevin's lack of co-operation. Situations like this are common, especially with strong-willed children. Even though Kevin was unwilling to discuss the matter, Dad remained calm; he did not start lecturing Kevin about hitting or about being stubborn. Dad recognized that Kevin was not willing to talk. Wisely, Dad did not insist. It is better to wait for Kevin to cool off before talking further. Dad will have more of Kevin's attention.

Zest for living must exist within yourself. It cannot come from outside sources. Your children learn this from you. Love your children unconditionally, and they will learn to do the same. Show each of your children how much you value her or him. A child should believe, 'No matter how tough the world out there gets, someone supports me.' That's what children need to deal with peer pressure effectively.

Guide children to think for themselves when they are young. Give them choices. Praise them when they make good decisions, show them where they could improve poor decisions, and help them see alternatives to their decisions and their behaviour. Teach them the power to choose their future.

Chapter 33

Hey, Teenagers! It is in Your Best Interest To Behave!

About a year ago I was the guest on a radio talk show where the host and I were speaking to listeners and taking calls about discipline and child behaviour. As usual, most callers had questions about young children. But then we received a call from a father of four teenagers. He had more of a comment than a question. He noted that most of the callers had concerns about children not listening and not obeying. He added how his teenagers were fairly well behaved because he had always approached discipline from a positive perspective and that he had always reasoned with his children about their good behaviour as well as their misconduct. He was encouraging the listeners to do the same. But then he added that this way of teaching children required a lot of hard work and commitment and some self-restraint at times.

After the call, the host and I began to talk more about discipline and teenagers. I explained that disciplining teenagers begins at about age four. You cannot begin at age fourteen.

The groundwork needs to be done early. Children need to learn about responsibility and privilege while they are young. I explained that the adolescent years are easier when parents and teens are willing to talk and listen to each other. Negotiation and compromise are often the key ingredients for teenager and parent survival. Then the host asked about my teenagers.

'Do you ever have any disagreements with your
    children?'
'Of course. My kids are normal.'
'Tell us about something you and one of your
    teenagers disagree about.'
'Well, right now my daughter and I are not agreeing
    about a concert she wants to go to. She enjoys
    going to concerts, and I allow her to go to most.
    But I am not too sure about this particular
    concert. I don't think she should go. We are
    still talking about this one.'
'What if you tell her she can't go?'
'She probably won't go.'
'What if she does?'
'I don't think she will.'
'Why not?'
'Because it is not in her best interest!'

It is *not* in her best interest to go to the concert. It *is* in her best interest to behave responsibly and make good decisions. That is how she keeps my trust. That is also how she keeps her freedom, privileges, spending money and car keys. I cannot stop her from going to the concert. She is the only one who can do that. But she knows that three hours at a concert she was told not to attend would not be worth it. She would lose my trust.

Teenagers need their parents' trust. They earn trust by being responsible. This sounds so simple, but I am always amazed by how teenagers and parents do not understand this. For some unknown reason, teenagers seem to build a communication wall between themselves and their parents. Many parents and adolescents have regular, ongoing conflicts and power struggles. They argue about everything. There is better way. Whenever I counsel with teenagers I explain this idea:

> 'This is the time in your life when you want to make your parents very happy. You want them to trust you. You want them to believe that you are a good student. You want to get good marks. You want to do a good job on your chores. You want to be polite and kind to your little brothers and sisters. You need to be home by the agreed time. You want your parents to think you are an extremely responsible person. Because when they think you behave responsibly, then they will trust you. Then good things will happen in your life. They will allow you to do more activities because they know they can trust you. You may not believe this, but your parents really do want to do nice things for you.'

I have had this talk with hundreds of adolescents over the years, and almost every one has reacted with the same expression: 'I never thought of it that way!' I do not think many parents think this way either. I am quick to remind these enlightened adolescents that change takes time. It will take time for them to change, but more importantly, it will take time for their parents to change.

If the relationship between teens and parents has been filled with power struggles and conflicts for months or years, it will take more than a few days of responsible behaviour to improve that relationship and build trust. Parents and teens need to remind each other to be patient and stay focused on positive behaviour and attitudes.

When children and teens behave properly, then it is up to parents to behave responsibly, too! Give your children encouragement and support. Look for small improvements at first. Acknowledge any step in the right direction, no matter how small. Talk with your teenagers and your younger children about the benefits of responsible behaviour. Do not forget to add that as a bonus, when you make good decisions and behave responsibly, you feel proud of yourself. Teach your children that happiness comes from the inside, from doing the right thing. That feeling will be helpful during adolescence and the rest of their lives.

Part VII

How to Enjoy Being a Parent

Chapter 34
Promise to Appreciate

Anthony doesn't pee in the refrigerator anymore. After reading about himself on page 4, he said he felt like doing it again just to get even with me for telling the story. Since his bladder capacity is considerably greater than it was ten years ago, I am trying to stay on his good side. We have made it to the fireworks for the past six years. I have learned how to keep stupid threats to myself. Leah eats like a superstar whenever we go out to dinner. She still orders a cheeseburger with chips and a small milk and one straw. I have stopped cursing in parking lots, almost.

Michael no longer has tantrums in the supermarket or anywhere else. He still loves chocolate. Mrs Ellis has not taken any more breaks from consistency. Her children are doing quite well in school and at home. Nancie will graduate from secondary school this year. She has not skipped classes to hide in her cupboard in four years, as far as we know.

You cannot accuse children of being boring. They will always think of something you are unprepared to handle. Being a parent is demanding; it requires countless sacrifices and continuous hard work. Fortunately, there are many rewards: the pride of achievement, the miracle of growth and development, the warmth and affection. If your children's misbehaviour is depriving you of these rewards, you are being cheated. Do not let this happen. You are doing the work without the glory. You deserve to enjoy your children.

Several years ago, I was at a school for profoundly handicapped children. When I got in my car to leave, I decided to write some notes. While I was working, an estate car drove in and parked in front of me. An elderly gentleman got out. He walked around to the back and opened the boot. He was struggling with something. Then I realized what it was – a wheelchair. He dragged it to the ground and locked it into position. He rolled the chair to the passenger side, opened the rear door, and reached deep inside. He emerged with his full-grown son in his arms. He placed his son's dangling torso in the chair, fastened the strap, and wheeled him into school.

My only thought was for my children. How many times had I silently complained about buckling Leah into her car seat? How often was I upset because her arms and legs did not move as quickly as I wanted? It was a painful but revitalizing insight. I made a vow: to appreciate and enjoy my children to the fullest.

All parents want to enjoy their children, but few parents get the enjoyment they deserve. It is easy to appreciate your children when they are co-operative and well behaved. You can spend your time and energy on pleasant endeavours. You do not have to yell and argue. It is difficult to enjoy your children when they misbehave. Misconduct creates tension.

Many parents avoid their children to escape the stress and irritated feelings. They send their children outside to play so they do not have to deal with them. They cannot wait until the children go to bed. They see their children as a burden and resent them. They hope for the day when their children leave home. This is a tragic waste of a precious opportunity. It can be avoided. Take time periodically to review these points:

Ten Principles to Practise

1. Pay off correct behaviour, not misbehaviour. Reinforce polite requests, not whining, teasing and tantrums. Reinforce calm discussions, not arguments and power struggles.

2. Think before you talk. Say what you mean. Mean what you say. Follow through. Give yourself visual reminders. Reward yourself for being consistent.

3. Expect good behaviour from your children. Children must know what you expect from them and what they can expect from you. When children can predict how you behave in given situations, they make better choices.

4. Children believe what you tell them. Coach your children on ways to be successful. Teach your children that effort is essential to success. Use plenty of encouragement. When you encourage your children, they will see that you have faith and confidence in them. Encouragement will help your children face situations with more confidence.

5. Anticipate problems. Tell them the rules in advance. Be specific. Be reasonable. Once you recognize a misbehaviour pattern, establish a plan. Spotlight success. Provide support and encouragement. Use charts and contracts to strengthen your plan.

6. Use punishments that teach decision making and accountability. Children survive reasonable punishments, such as restriction and time-out. Do not punish when you are angry, or to get even. Relating punishment to your child's decisions teaches responsibility.

7. Begin teaching responsibility and decision-making when your children are young. Prepare your children to live in the real world. Be strict but positive. Children need

limits and structure, ground rules and consistency. Children see these qualities as an expression of your love and concern.

8. Love your children regardless of their behaviour. Focus on your children's positive qualities. Teach your children to seek self-reward – to feel good about doing the right thing. Look for praiseworthy decisions. Teach your children to like themselves, to understand their weaknesses and accept their faults. Use yourself as an example. When they learn to admit their shortcomings to others, their weaknesses will have less power in their lives.

9. Support yourself, even when others sit in judgment. Do not let your children push your buttons. Be strong. Control your own behaviour to be a good model. Your children learn from you.

10. Provide a healthy and pleasant family climate. Emphasize each other's strengths. Accept each other's weaknesses. Talk about values and goals. Your children will learn to come to you with their problems. This will come in handy when they are teenagers.

Final Thoughts

Being a successful parent is hard work. Developing well-behaved children requires courage and patience. Trust yourself: you know what is best for your children. Concentrate on the real issues: mental health, happiness, self-respect and love of others.

Some parents believe that love alone will create delightful children. Love is essential, but it does not guarantee good behaviour. Misbehaviour is not pleasant. There is a better way. Practise the ideas presented in this book.

You have a right to enjoy being a parent. Do not let your children's misbehaviour keep you from enjoying them. Take action. Plan to change the misbehaviour and then have fun. Laugh and play and get involved with your children. It will keep you feeling young. These are the most valuable years of your life.

Index

A

achievements 4
activity incentives 42–3
ADD (attention deficit disorder) 234
ADHD (attention deficit
    hyperactivity disorder) 234
anger 5, 199–205
   management strategies 201–5
   parental 117–20
   as payoff 125–6
   and spanking 145–6
   triggers 200, 205
anticipation 63–5
arguments 176–85
aspirations, parents 4
attention deficit disorder (ADD)
   234
attention deficit hyperactivity
   disorder (ADHD) 234
attention
   kinds of 188–9
   negative, as a reward 189–90
   positive 189, 190, 192
   as a reward 188–9
   withholding 191–2
attention-seeking
   excessive 187–8
   and misbehaviour 188
authority, and power 178–9, 185

B

behaviour *see also* misbehaviour
   changing 12, 26
   and choices 61–2
   effect of environment 22
   good, reinforcing 52
   good, and special events 41–2
   good, spotlighting 33–4
   learned 22, 23–5
   modelling (copying) 19–21
   praising 37
   principles to practice 267–8
   problems 4–5
blended families 246
breathing and anger control 201–2
bribery 107–8, 112–13
budgeting, teaching 221
button pushing 115–21, 182, 183, 191
   defending against 118–21
   rewards for 116–17
   time out, use of 148, 150

C

change, and successful parenting 6
changes in society 10
chart-making guidelines 57
charts 49–52
   developing 51–2
   reasons to use 56
   and school behaviour 52–3

checklists 53–4
  and homework 231
children
  appreciation of 266
  learning behaviour 11
  listening to 251–3
  making decisions 16
  pressures on 9–10
  self–control 15
  and trauma 208
children's behaviour, affecting
      parents 30
choices, and consequences 61–2
chores 217–18
  and allowance 218–20, 222
clarifying (feelings) 253–4
compromise 215
confidence
  parents 9, 182, 183
  and peer pressure 250
conflict, between siblings 213–15
consequences 59–62 *see also*
      incentives
  and decision making 60–2
  enforceable 61
  negative 60–2
  positive 60–2
  reality 62
  reasonable 61
  specific 61
consistency 6, 87–90 *see also*
      inconsistency
  and difficult children 236
  after divorce 246–7
  and follow through 93–5
  importance of 102–3
  maintaining 97–103
  between parents 95–6
  and patience 100
  priority behaviours 98–9
  and punishment 127
  reminders 99
  and rules 60
consumerism, teaching 221
contracts 27, 49, 54–5
reasons to use 56
copying *see* modelling
correction, verbal 179–81
credit cards 221
criticism 73
current accounts 221

D

decision making
  by children

and consequences 60–2
and expectations 59
difficult children 233–6
  and ADD/ADHD 234
  and consistency 236
  early intervention 235
  planning ahead for 234–6
disappointments, overcoming 84–5
discipline 6
  and cooperation 14–15
  and punishment 13
  purpose of 14
  and teaching decision making 14
divorce 237–47
  and school 239–40, 246
  children's feelings about 237–45
  importance of consistency 246–7

E

embarrassment and punishment 126
emotional intelligence 210
encouragement 37, 38
environment, and behaviour 22
excuses, and misbehaviour 111–12
expectations 59–62
  acting to 36–7
  clarifying 52, 55
  enforceable 60
  reasonable 60
  specific 59–60
experience, and behaviour 22
extended families 246–7
extinction, of behaviour 109–11

F

families
  blended 246
  extended 246–7
family climate 75–8
  comparisons 79–80
  and humour 76–7
  and motivation 75–6
feelings, expressing 253–4

G

goals 218
  parents 4
good behaviour *see* behaviour, good
guilt 182
  parental 117–19

H

happiness 268
hard work, encouraging 38
homework 227–31
  use of checklists 231

incentives 230–1
motivation 230–1
successful strategies 228–30
humour 76–7

I

ignoring misbehaviour 191–2
improvements, encouraging 38
incentives 50–2, 74 *see also*
            consequences
    activity 42–3
    for children over twelve years 46–7
    for children under twelve years 44–5
    and homework 230–1
    tangible 43
inconsistency 5 *see also* consistency
    of threats 90–1
intelligence, emotional 210
interest and motivation 74–5
interests, knowledge of child's 78–9

L

learned behaviour 23–5
listening
    to children 251–3
    and trust 251–3
love 9, 37, 268

M

media violence 209–10
mental health 268
misbehaviour 266, 268–9 *see also*
            behaviour
    and attention –seeking 188
    learned 107–13
    managing 193–6
    motivation for 194
    patterns 193–4
    redirecting 28
    weakening 34–5
mistakes, learning from 38
modelling (copying)
    and child abuse 21
    parents as example 19–21
money, value of 220–2
motivation 35, 71–5
    and contracts 55
    external 71–2
    and homework 230–1
    and interest 74–5
    internal 71–2
    for misbehaviour 194

P

parental anger 117–19
parental guilt 117–20

parenthood, enjoying 266, 268–9
parenting behaviour
    learning of 8, 11
    training 9, 10
parents
    anger 5
    aspirations 4
    behaviour, affecting children 30
    confidence 9
    goals 4
    help from other parents 7
    inconsistency 5
    as models 6, 19–21
    openness 10
    passive behaviour 5
    patience 10
    practise 11
    reactions 5
    successful 6
passive behaviour, parents 5
patience 5, 10
    and consistency 100
payoffs 29, 111
    and learned behaviour 27–8
peer pressure 249–57
    and confidence 250
planning 5, 63–70
    for difficult children 234–6
    for improved behaviour 65–70
positive attention 192
positive feedback 33–9, 38, 111,
            128–9, 130–2
    compared with punishment 131–2
positive focus 6
positive reinforcement 215
power and authority 178–9, 185
power struggles 176–8
power-seeking children 176
prevention 5
priorities 60
priority behaviours, and consistency
            98–9
priority misbehaviour and time–out
            154–6, 162–3
privileges, and responsibility 218
problem solving by children 254–7
punishment 5, 123–32
    and anger 125–6
    compared with positive feedback
            131–2
    and consistency 127
    and control 26, 133–4
    effect on parents 133–4
    and embarrassment 126

enforcement 134–5
explaining 135–6
proper use of 133–9
questions to ask 129–30
reality consequences 136
reasonable 127
use of restrictions 138–9
size of 136–7
timing 128
pushing buttons *see* button pushing

R

reality consequences 62
respect, for other person 214, 215
responsibility 22, 61–2
age appropriate 224–5
encouraging 38
parents as models 6
and privileges 218
teaching about 223
teaching with charts 52
restrictions, proper use of 138–9
retaliation, cycle of 182–3
revenge 181–3
rewards 35, 50–1
and negative attention 189–90
of being a parent 266
role playing, and anger management
202
rules 59–62
and consistency 60

S

savings 221
school
behaviour and charts 52–3
and divorce 239–40, 246
violence 207–8
self-discipline 22
self-esteem 6, 35
and disappointments 84–5
and motivation 81–5
and respect 83
and spanking 143, 144
self-motivation 35 *see also*
motivation
self-respect 268
self-reward 36
shaping behaviour 72–4
shopping 64–5
sibling conflict 213–15
sibling rivalry 3
spanking 141–46
in anger 145–6
as external control 142
impulsive use of 143–5

planned approach 145
and self-esteem 143, 144, 145
special events and good behaviour
41–2
stall statements 92–3
success 4
and internal motivation 72–4

T

tangible incentive 43
tantrums 23–5, 108–10
teasing 108–9
teenagers 15, 250–2
and contracts 55
and friends 251
listening to 251–3
thinking for themselves 254–7
and trust 259–62
testing, by children 101–2
threats, inconsistency of 90–1
time warnings 91–2
time-out 147–64
and behaviour improvement 161–2
charting 159–61, 164
and chores 159
coming out of 158–9
delayed 170
difficult situations 170–1
explaining to children 156–8
guidelines 173–174
and priority misbehaviour 154–6,
162–3
refusal to go 165–8
and removal of privileges 167–8
and removal of toys 166–8
setting for 151–3
time spent in 153–4
for tiny tots 171–2
for two children 171
times of day, difficult 101
timing, of new plans 100–1
trauma and children 208
trust
encouraging 38
and teenagers 259–62

V

violence
in the media 209–10
at school 207–8

W

warnings 91–2
whining 108–9
work, value of 217

Also available from Vermilion

☐	Adolescence	0091891620	£8.99
☐	How to be a Better Parent	0091889723	£8.99
☐	New Toddler Taming	0091875285	£12.99
☐	Positive Parenting	0749315016	£6.99
☐	The Golden Rules of Parenting	0091882850	£6.99

FREE POST AND PACKING

Overseas customers allow £2.00 per paperback

ORDER:

BY PHONE: 01624 677237

**BY POST: Random House Books
C/o Bookpost, PO Box 29, Douglas
Isle of Man, IM99 1BQ**

BY FAX: 01624 670923

BY EMAIL: bookshop@enterprise.net

Cheques (payable to Bookpost) and credit cards accepted

Prices and availability subject to change without notice.
Allow 28 days for delivery.
When placing your order, please mention if you do not wish to receive
any additional information

www.randomhouse.co.uk